Collectors' LOT

Collectors' LOT

A Nation of Collectors

CHRISSIE KRAVCHENKO

CHANNEL 4 BOOKS

First published in 1998 by Channel 4 Books
an imprint of Macmillan Publishers Ltd
25 Eccleston Place
London SW1W 9NF
and Basingstoke.

Associated companies throughout the world.

ISBN 0 7522 2196 5

9 8 7 6 5 4 3 2 1

A CIP catalogue record for this book is available from the British Library.

Commissioning Editor: Charlie Carman
Editor: Emma Tait
Original photography by Ed Schneider
(detailed credits given on page 160)
Colour reproduction by Speedscan Limited
Printed in England by Bath Press Limited

This book accompanies the television series *Collectors' Lot*
made by Two Four Productions for Channel 4.
Executive producers: Charles Wace and Jill Lourie
Producers: Sadie Hennessy, Annabel Hibbard and Melanie Leach

CONTENTS

> *"I couldn't help it ~ I can resist everything except Temptation"*
> OSCAR WILDE

— Foreword —

As I write this there have been two series of *Collectors' Lot* and we're about to embark on the third. That means nearly seven hundred people, so far, have had the chance to show off their collections and we've still only scratched the surface.

Over past years the series has unearthed a treasure trove of items that mirror changing social trends. To me, *Collectors' Lot*'s appeal also lies in the fact that it is an archive of people's very personal memories. As regular viewers will know, *Collectors' Lot* is all about real people whose collections may (or may not) be priceless but have an intrinsic, sometimes highly sentimental, value to their owner. This book revisits some of the most memorable collections and proves why from Perth to Penzance we are a nation of collectors.

I hope you'll enjoy seeing some of the most unforgettable prized possessions.

Happy collecting!

Debbie Thrower.

Introduction

I discovered my own hoarding instinct during my student days. I enjoyed making clothes and used to trawl through junk shops looking for interesting old fabrics. I felt the need to rescue any handmade lace or 1930s dresses I came across – and there were plenty of them going cheap in the early 1970s. When, many years later, I opened my own shop, I squirreled away certain bits and pieces instead of putting them in the window. These weren't usually expensive things, but items that were part of the story I had decided to tell through my collection. So I have to confess that the shop didn't only earn a living, but also fed my delight in period clothing and bijoux.

Everyone who has contributed to this book has his or her own reasons for collecting. One of the challenges has been to reconcile the differences between collectors within the covers of one, fairly short, book. So the book doesn't attempt to be a comprehensive or exhaustive directory of the series. Rather, it explores some of the more quirky areas. Why, for example, an old powder compact or toaster might be of value. What to do with the collection of old marbles that your uncle left you. How you might recognise a Victorian Christmas card and what you'd have to pay for it these days. At the same time, in the more traditional areas such as pottery or jewellery, we get an insight into what attracts a keen and experienced collector.

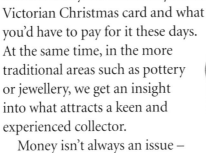

Money isn't always an issue – some items are worthless to all but the collector, others are of sentimental value and never likely to be put up for sale. Often collectors value artistic technical brilliance above monetary value.

At times, it's been a daunting task to talk to so many experts, yet it's been a privilege too. Their skill and knowledge was a reminder that there is no substitute for the kind of experience that can spot a treasure, even if it lies unappreciated at the bottom of a box full of jumble.

My own theory is that collecting not only fulfils a human instinct to make sense of the world that we live in, but also that it is one of the ways in which an adult plays. There is plenty of fun and many opportunities to socialise when searching for a piece to add to your collection, buying your find and researching your field.

The amount of time a collector spends on his or her collection varies greatly – for some it will always be a hobby, for others it is central to life. Yet the same phrases crop up again and again: 'the hunter-gatherer instinct', 'in the genes', 'the fun of the chase', 'human curiosity'. A few people confessed, with a degree of self-mockery, that they view their habit as an eccentric 'disease' that needs to be kept under control. For a very small number it has, at one time or another, become a compulsion. For others it has provided a lifeline at a difficult time.

I haven't had much opportunity recently to toy with my own modest collections, but wherever I go an in-built antenna draws my eye to unusual items. Like many people, I can't afford to buy those sought after pieces that cost a small fortune these days, but we can all feel enriched, at least for an afternoon, as we wander round one of the museums opened by a dedicated collector.

As horologist Kim-John Webb so succinctly pointed out, 'I think collecting is what makes the world go round. If someone wants to find out about anything there's bound to be a collector somewhere who has done the research, tying one design to another, looking at factory patents, shedding light on things. A certain amount of eccentricity is a prerequisite, but the knowledge can be shared.' The result, ultimately, is a wonderful legacy.

Chrissie Kravchenko

CHAPTER ONE

A Touch of Class

The Decorative Arts

Our homes can reveal a great deal about our tastes and personalities. Design has evolved throughout the twentieth century, but the quality of good style is always welcome. So now we choose objects from the past to add an interesting dimension to our living spaces.

A t the beginning of the twentieth century, most families were hard pressed to stay healthy in overcrowded conditions, so style was something of a luxury. Fortunately for collectors, the better off families kept the wheels of industry turning by buying the wonderful array of tableware, ornaments, lamps and other decorative wares that adorned their homes. Talented artists, craftspeople and artisans kept customers supplied with quality Art Nouveau, Edwardian and Art Deco objects, right up until the outbreak of World War II.

These items are now cherished by collectors who love the quality and novelty of twentieth-century decorative arts. As demand has outstripped availability, prices for the best pieces have risen. So collectors, ever adaptable, have turned their attention to post-World War II designs, which by and large are more available and more modestly priced. How collectable these will become isn't easy to predict. Taste and style evolve. It's interesting to note, however, that some of the objects cherished as decorative arts today, Clarice Cliff's pottery for instance, were mass produced and cheap to buy.

COLLECTOR'S TIP

'Leave your card with trusted dealers so they can call you if something special comes in!'

MAJOR DONALD WELSH

A CENTURY OF DECORATIVE ARTS

The term decorative arts is used to describe a vast range of collectables. Some are old enough to be antiques; others were recently crafted. One of the main criteria is that they have to be more than basic utility products. Though some are practical items, such as drinking glasses, jugs or teapots, there has to be something special about the artistry and design in order for them to become collectable.

The materials an object is made from are clues used by today's collectors to date a piece. Traditional materials – gold, silver, wood, glass and ceramics – have been used throughout the past two centuries, but in the nineteenth century unconventional materials appeared, which have since gone out of fashion. These included tortoiseshell, various animal bones and papier mâché. Later, you begin to find plastics and aluminium.

Scent bottles, small porcelain statues, lamps, vases and picture frames would all be included in a decorative arts sale. So would items of jewellery by designers better known for their household items. One such designer is the French glass-maker René Lalique (1860–1945), who is famous for his lamps and scent bottles. Dating his work can be difficult, but a good general rule is to look at the colour of the glass – earlier pieces usually have a greyish tint, while his post-war glass is often clearer.

Anyone building a collection should know how to recognise quality. Barring a few exceptions, things that were badly designed and cheaply made, or that mimic a past era, are going to be less attractive than items of contemporary design and good workmanship.

Design may be a matter of taste, but each era has its innovators. It is the work of this elite band of artisans that is most highly prized, and which dictates the instantly recognisable style of each era. Some of the designs are so popular that they're reproduced in great numbers. Many pieces will have marks or makers' names to help distinguish the originals, but an expert will know by looking at an object whether it is 'right'.

An English Bakelite cocktail shaker with silver plated mounts. This was one of a range made in the mid-1930s, using the same colours as Bakelite telephones of the day. The cap rotates to reveal recipes for eight different cocktails.

COLLECTING DECORATIVE ARTS

The challenge in this field is to sort out who have been the key designers during recent decades. Some collectors, however, are drawn to the cheap and cheerful for what it has to say about the everyday past – these collectors love all things kitsch and by incorporating them into their decor create their own inimitable style.

Volumes, it seems, have been written about the decorative arts, but here a few collectors have been selected to represent the main collecting areas. Ceramics and glass are vast fields in themselves – distinctive styles were developed during each era. But there are general tips, which will help you to recognise quality.

The first thing to look at when judging any piece, be it a lamp, a trinket or a piece of pottery, is the design. Does it immediately bring to mind a particular era? The next question is about quality. Has a lot of expense gone into its production? For some things, such as a metal candlestick, you might need to check that it is sturdy, while for others, like a fine porcelain dish, a light translucent quality is desirable.

One of a limited edition, this paperweight was made by the UK firm Whitefriars in 1970 to commemorate the 350th anniversary of the Pilgrim Fathers' voyage on the Mayflower.

'My tip is buy what you really like yourself. Don't always be influenced by people who say you should only get a perfect this or that,' says the established collector and dealer Judith Howard. Though she showed her collection of Valentine cards on *Collectors' Lot* (*see page 139*), her passion is pottery. 'When you consider it, we don't really own anything, we're custodians. We borrow things during the time they're in our possession. So a chip doesn't matter to me, as a collector. If a thing's not perfect, I'm glad, because it means I'll be able to afford something beautiful that might otherwise have been too expensive. Life isn't about getting your money back. If you love something you don't want to sell it on anyway.'

Collectors usually start by amassing items that vary wildly in quality and then refine their tastes. 'I only buy interesting cocktail shakers now,' says collector and expert Simon Khachadourian, 'those with some artistic or humorous merit. Otherwise you can end up with junk, which isn't nice to look at. The outrageous symbols of design you found in the 1920s and 1930s wouldn't happen now. There was a whole design theme from about 1900 to 1950.'

EGYPTIANA
Richard Lowe

'I'll collect anything with a camel or Nefertiti on it,' says Egyptiana collector Richard Lowe of London, who enjoys what he calls 'clutterphilia'. He's a mural painter and display artist by trade, and has made his flat into a living portfolio.

'My flat was just a modern concrete shell, but now I have an Aboriginal living room, a Kashmiri bedroom and an Egyptian hallway, bathroom and kitchen. My parents took me to Egypt when I was sixteen, which is an impressionable age.

'Twenty years ago, when I started my Egyptiana collection, it was considered very kitsch. It's quite fashionable now. Most of the stuff I collect was made as souvenirs for early Thomas Cook tourists. I've got watercolours of sunsets behind the pyramids, the ones you imagine were painted by Edwardian spinsters. I've also got a lot of Noretaki china with palm trees and camel motifs. My collection is based on aesthetic rather than historic interest. For example, I don't read hieroglyphics, but I do have Egyptian-style ducks in my bath.

'I think collecting is either in the blood or it's not. I'm somebody who will wander on a beach and pick up shells. I can't pass a skip without rummaging through it.

'I haven't been back to Egypt since I was sixteen – I don't want to spoil the memories.'

Throwaway items can become fashionable and valuable over time. China by the Japanese firm Noretaki was made for the European market in the nineteenth and early twentieth centuries. They produced Egyptian style porcelain, decorated with sunsets, Bedouin tents and camels. Not all of it was of equal quality – the earlier hand-painted crockery is far more desirable than the transfer printed pieces made since the turn of the twentieth century.

Although Richard is happy to buy a cheap souvenir, it must have some artistic merit. If it's made by local people in their own style he's impressed. He would see the creativity of a tin toy made out of a coke can, but something churned out using an old idea isn't going to have credibility. It's a matter of learning to recognise artistic merit.

Part of Richard Lowe's collection of Egyptiana is displayed in the hallway of his London home.

Cocktail Shakers

Simon Khachadourian

'AT 5AM EVERY FRIDAY, before going to work in the City, I used to scour Bermondsey market for affordable pieces.' This habit led trainee ship-broker Simon Khachadourian so far astray, that he's become the world expert on collectable cocktail shakers.

'In 1977 I spotted my first Tells-U-How shaker, which is typical of 1930s novelty style. It has windows all around it with sixteen cocktail recipes behind – Manhattan, Palm Beach, Martini and so on. I paid £30, which

was a lot of money then, but I was fascinated by it. It's one of the most popular shakers, the idea was copied by different makers. It was designed and made by Asprey, so it can't have been inexpensive when new. It would sell today for around £1,500–£1,800. There were eight or nine novelty shakers made by Asprey in the 1930s, a lovely set to collect. The rarest is the Thirst Extinguisher, in the shape of a fire extinguisher, the others include a Dumb-Bell, a Ship's Lantern, and a Champagne Magnum.

Simon is seen here with some of his 400 cocktail shakers, including the Thirst Extinguisher (left), the Dumb-Bells (right) and other Asprey and Cartier shakers. One way of judging a shaker is by handling it – they should feel solid and heavy.

It took a long time to find them all, I'd go to auctions, antique markets or buy from other collectors – wherever I could.

I have that unfortunate collecting gene, probably inherited from my father. He was an academic, and collected illuminated Armenian manuscripts, so I grew up with interesting and unusual things. People are either collectors by nature or they're not. It's partly to do with the thrill of the chase, from recognising the worth of something that others have overlooked.'

COLLECTING COCKTAIL SHAKERS

Collectors look for the novelty shakers made in the USA and Britain from the late 1920s. In 1926 the world's first novelty shaker, in the shape of a golf-bag, was patented in the USA by George Berry. From then on, many designers and manufacturers produced them on both sides of the Atlantic. They were still being made in the 1950s, but by then they were past their best. You're unlikely to find a good novelty shaker, made in the heyday of the 1920s or 1930s, for below £200, and it could cost considerably more.

Most shakers were made of non-precious metals, but you'll also find older, more discreetly designed silver ones. Collectors favour the humorous novelty shakers, which are typical of the between-the-wars chic.

You can see the shaker collection and other twentieth-century *objets de luxe* at Simon's new gallery, The Pullman, in St James's.

A rare complete Zeppelin cocktail set, made in Germany around 1930 for export.

PLASTIC

Moulded plastics were the poor relations of the decorative arts world until fairly recently. Although plastics were expensive when they were first developed, they've had an image problem – being associated with cheap, disposable goods – since they became more widely used in the 1930s. But there are collectors who appreciate the fun and colour of this versatile material.

Plastic is a truly twentieth-century collectable, although the earliest plastics were developed in Victorian times. Those early celluloids were more brittle than later plastics, so little has survived, but once you know what to look for you'll come across small toys, pieces of jewellery, combs and other oddities made from it. Often they look and feel like ivory, but don't be tempted to wash them – they don't react well to water!

The sturdy plastics that were on the market by the 1930s were welcomed by designers, who loved the potential they gave to create colourful, practical pieces. While some objects, such as the bright and bold Art Deco designs, have been valued for many years, others, perhaps with less obvious charm, have increased in value much more slowly. The most collectable will be the innovative designs of each period, the ones that are easy to date by the look of them.

Prices vary as many pieces attract collectors in more than one field. For example, a camera collector might not value a Bakelite camera that highly, because it's a common model, whereas a collector of plastics would pay a substantial sum for it. There's plenty to look at, it's simply a matter of taste.

This waterdome, from Michelle Morgan's Marilyn Monroe collection (see pages 56–7) was made recently by a firm in the USA and endorsed by the Marilyn Monroe Trust. This means that a proportion of the profits will go to the charities mentioned in Marilyn's will.

CERAMICS

When European potters saw the white porcelain imported from China in the seventeenth century they were impressed. The pots had a translucent quality and more delicate appearance than European earthenware, yet they were strong. In the eighteenth century, early attempts to copy the technique resulted in 'soft-paste' porcelain. Many of the rarest and most valuable pots are made of soft-paste. Collectors value them, but they weren't as sturdy as their Chinese equivalents and so broke easily. Later, techniques improved to produce 'hard-paste' and bone china.

Soft-paste rarely looks as perfect as hard-paste. The colours have often run, the glaze can have a slightly bubbly quality, it's more grainy and less glass-like than hard-paste. Yet pottery experts treasure these old pieces and it isn't unusual for a good example to cost thousands of pounds, though not all are so expensive. It's important for a collector to learn the difference between the two, as most fakes of soft-paste are in fact hard-paste. Soft-paste feels 'warmer' to the touch and after handling a few pieces it's reasonably easy to tell the difference. Even so, some of the most expensive mistakes are made by pottery collectors, even experienced ones. It's a huge and complicated subject.

There's a lot of fun to be had looking for impressed or printed signatures, but you soon learn that you can't really rely on them to be accurate. This is especially true when looking at pots made in the nineteenth century. An experienced collector will look first at

Two 9 in (23 cm) plates by Myott, Son & Co. The plate on the left is 1930s, the simple leaf motif being typical of the time.

the shape and style, then at the type of clay and the condition of a pot before looking for a mark.

Up to the 1850s, most firms didn't mark comprehensively – so if you have no other way of recognising something special, you might miss a lovely piece. However, if you get a feeling that you're looking at something interesting, knowing what mark to expect might just clinch it. Marks can offer valuable clues and you'll find books devoted to them in both shops and through collectors' clubs. Some marks to look for are: a diamond shaped registration mark, which appeared on pottery between 1842 and 1883; 'England', which was used after 1891 when an act of parliament ordered that the country of origin be stamped on to pottery; and 'Made in Britain' or 'Made in England', which were used from around 1910.

As rare and valuable antique pottery becomes hard to find, people are turning to interesting pieces made after World War II. Designs from the 1950s through to present-day studio pottery are becoming more sought after. Look out for the best quality made at the time, in styles that are typical of the decade. By this time, pieces were more consistently marked.

During World War II, the factories at Stoke-on-Trent produced decorative ware for export only. Most of this used traditional floral and figurative designs that had been popular since the last century. At home, people used the plainer 'Utility' ceramics, which reflected a time of austerity. They were usually made of earthenware and used little colour. Decoration was subtle and followed 1930s style.

As soon as restrictions were lifted in the 1950s, we begin to see the splashes of colour and new shapes that look so typical to us today. Potters were influenced by successful artists, such as Pablo Picasso, Henry Moore and Jean Arp. They experimented with shape and the technique of silk-screen printing on to pottery over the glaze, which gave it a distinct texture. For the first time it became possible for potters to transfer print on to the inside of curved surfaces, so you find the insides of basins and bowls decorated all over. Collectors love anything that sits comfortably in its time – and for the 1950s and 1960s that meant experimentation with the abstract, through shapes and colour.

- Three Poole pottery vases, designed by Truda Adams and painted by (from the top) Marjorie Batt, Marjorie Evans and Phillis Ryall.

All of us collect pottery, even if we only use it to eat off. Every purchase, whether it's from a charity shop or from the local art school's degree show, is an opportunity to add to our collection. As many a collector has found, it can become the habit of a lifetime.

COALPORT CHINA
Ivor Southorn

Coalport is a Shropshire pottery that started in 1785. The firm went out of business briefly in 1926, but reopened and has been going ever since. In the nineteenth century it had a reputation for producing fine tableware, such as its printed blue-and-white porcelain and its flower encrusted 'Dresden style' pottery.

'Everyone here eats off Coalport. Even the dog drinks from a Coalport mug,' says Ivor Southorn, hotelier – and owner of the biggest Coalport china collection in the world.

'When I was nine, I went with my father to the disused Coalport factory in Ironbridge, near my home. The new owners wanted to dispose of a warehouse full of plaster moulds that were on the site. My family made clay pipes, so we were offered them.

'There were thousands of moulds, because when you made a teapot for instance, you needed one mould for the pot, one for the lid, one for the handle and one for the spout. I looked inside one of the moulds at the designs and carvings and thought "By Jove, whoever did that was a clever chap".

'We took them and stored them. And, I'm afraid, me and my four brothers would sometimes smash them for chalk when, say, we wanted to mark out a hopscotch pitch.

'But I never stopped thinking the designs were beautiful. When I grew up, I started collecting Coalport and couldn't stop. I'd buy plates, jugs, vases – some of them very old. The early ones are very colourful. You can't make them like that now; maybe because you can't get the artists. I've bought Coalport instead of paying the electricity and gas bills.

'I'll go a long way to collect. In 1897, fifty vases were made for Queen Victoria's diamond jubilee, specifically for sale in the USA. I flew to New York and bought one. I paid £3,000; it's probably worth £20,000 now.

'Profit has never come into it, for me. I've only ever sold one or two bits. I love giving talks and showing the collection to people and letting them handle the original Coalport. Nothing should be put away. All nice things should be shown.'

COLLECTOR'S TIP

'In the nineteenth century Sampson of Paris made copies of virtually any collectable pottery of the day. The Sampson marks were slightly different to the originals. The fakes are collectable in their own right today, though they're not as expensive as the real thing.'

Egg-cups
Isobel Whatrup

'THE FASCINATION FOR ME is the history which surrounds the egg-cups and the variety of materials they're made of,' says Isobel Whatrup of Kent, who has more than 2,000 examples in her collection.

'The earliest known egg-cups are silver and date from around 50 AD. They were found in the ruins of Pompeii. I have a "slag" egg-cup made from "end of the day" steelworks material mixed with glass to make an attractive colour. At the other end of the spectrum, I have some sparkling quality lead crystal ones.

'I've learned so much through collecting. For example, a bronze Arts and Crafts egg-

Amongst Isobel's favourite egg-cups are a Meissen, Spode, Worcester (First Period) and Bristol hard-paste (1770). In the cabinets you may spot onyx, jade, Art Deco, Dalton (blue and white) and crystal glass.

cup taught me how this movement affected late nineteenth-century poetry and furniture.

'It would be lovely to fill gaps in the collection. I have a Clarice Cliff egg-cup stand with a cockerel, which has three egg-cups missing. My dearest wish is to have a Tunbridge-ware egg-cup.'

COLLECTING EGG-CUPS

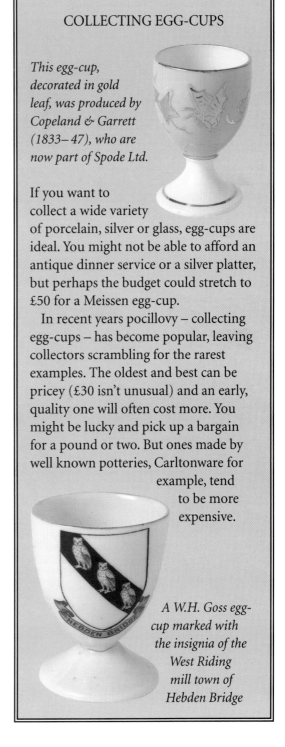

This egg-cup, decorated in gold leaf, was produced by Copeland & Garrett (1833–47), who are now part of Spode Ltd.

If you want to collect a wide variety of porcelain, silver or glass, egg-cups are ideal. You might not be able to afford an antique dinner service or a silver platter, but perhaps the budget could stretch to £50 for a Meissen egg-cup.

In recent years pocillovy – collecting egg-cups – has become popular, leaving collectors scrambling for the rarest examples. The oldest and best can be pricey (£30 isn't unusual) and an early, quality one will often cost more. You might be lucky and pick up a bargain for a pound or two. But ones made by well known potteries, Carltonware for example, tend to be more expensive.

A W.H. Goss egg-cup marked with the insignia of the West Riding mill town of Hebden Bridge

EGG-CUPS
Anneka Reay

Anneka Reay, aged eleven, started collecting early. 'My mum bought an egg-cup for me just before I was born. Now I collect the eggs from our chickens and ducks before I go to school. And I collect egg-cups.

'My parents stopped off at an antiques fair when I was seven and the first thing I saw was an egg-cup. They encouraged me to collect something so I wouldn't get bored.

'At car boot sales, people know me now and look out for egg-cups for me. I've got more choosy recently. I look at the bottoms now, as well as the patterns! One of my favourites is a mid-Victorian double-ended egg-cup. Another is a little cow with a nice expression. I paid £9 for a perfect Sooty egg-cup from Keele Street Pottery, which is quite collectable.

'I already have four Spitting Image egg-cups. I found a Diana one, but it was £30 and chipped, so I didn't get it. I've got some Royal Worcester and a Coalport one.

'Everyone buys them for me, and I've made friends with lots of people because of my egg cups.'

Anneka is shown here with her favourite egg-cups: the twin tigers flank (from the left) Sooty, Jersey Cow and Dismal Desmond. The Clarice Cliff cup was given to her by Sue Cook on Collectors' Lot.

TEAPOTS
Edward Bramah

When tea leaves were first brought to Britain from China at the end of the seventeenth century the same ships brought teapots made of Yixing ('ee-ching') stoneware or hard-paste porcelain. Once European potters got the hang of making hard-paste, they too began to produce a dazzling display of decorative and novelty teapots. One collector who has enjoyed buying them for over forty years is Edward Bramah.

'In my time I've been a tea planter, factory worker, shipper, broker, buyer, tea blender and taster, as well as having an interest in the ceramics of tea. I thought it appropriate to tell that story in my collection. I collected my purchases as props – you can't tell your story without your exhibits. I think the knowledge is important. I'm fascinated by all things to do with tea and coffee, especially in the evolutionary machinery of how to make these beverages, so if I see anything to do with this I'm drawn to buy it.'

Teapots have always presented problems for potters. They are made in one of two ways. Either they're thrown on a wheel and the spout and handle are added later, or they're made in a mould. Both methods produced stress lines, so the constant challenge is to design a teapot that doesn't leak or fracture when heated, but looks delicate and is not too heavy.

Collectors will come across them at fairs, most of them made this century. There are plenty around because some successful designs have been reproduced from the old moulds. Prices depend on the quality of the porcelain and the decoration. A rare, quality teapot can cost between £5,000 and £10,000 from a specialist shop.

This rare Meissen teapot, dating from around 1740, is an early example of European hard-paste. The underglaze is a blue scale pattern. From the Bramah collection.

GLASS

Glass-making has always been a prized art, and no wonder when you consider the awesome processes involved. Glass-making techniques were developed in ancient times: blowing, pressing, rolling, casting and drawing. In Egypt, glass beads dating back to the fifth millennium BC have been found. By the time of the Ptolemies, around 300 BC, there was a glassworks in Alexandria that exported around the ancient world.

Yet up until the nineteenth century, in Europe, blowing was the standard way to shape an object. After that, ancient ways of pressing and moulding glass were rediscovered and adapted to new styles. Mechanical pressing of glass was a cheaper and faster method than blowing, which meant that glass was used more widely in the home from the mid-nineteenth century, not only for tableware and decorative objects, but also as throw away containers for food and drink.

Because a mould could be made to produce a decorative finish, more labour intensive methods became quite rare in Victorian times. You won't find much cut glass, for instance, until the late nineteenth century, when there was a revival in the technique. Glass artists, inspired by the Arts and Crafts and Art Nouveau movements, wanted to show off their artistry in a backlash against mechanised production.

Glass can be a daunting subject. Perhaps this is why, until recently, it has been largely undervalued as a collectable. It can be difficult to date, too, because it isn't always marked and even old glass can look remarkably fresh. There are clues to help, if you know what to look for, but it isn't a straightforward science. New pieces are reproduced in old styles, too, so a budding collector needs to learn to pick out familiar shapes and techniques before spending a lot of money. Very old and valuable glass can easily stand unnoticed by someone unfamiliar with the subtle decoration. It doesn't stand out in the same way as a colourful Art Nouveau lamp, or a large contemporary art glass vase.

Carnival glass, so-called because it was cheap enough to be given away as prizes at fairs, was made in England and the USA from 1895–1925. It is moulded, coloured glass with an iridescent appearance.

At the beginning of the century, it seemed that all the best designs were coming from overseas. In France, Emile Gallé (1846–1904) was a leading exponent of Art Nouveau style, and his glass-making techniques were taken up in the USA by Louis Comfort Tiffany (1848–1933). Tiffany's iridescent glassworks were known by the trademark 'Favrile', which is French for 'handmade'. Up to the 1930s another Frenchman, René Lalique was the most influential maker – these days people clamour to collect anything by him or in his style. His company, Cristal Lalique was established in 1909. It continued after his death and those later pieces were signed simply 'Lalique', whereas the ones made while Lalique was alive were signed 'R. Lalique'.

Some of the most popular and attractive moulded glass of the 1930s came in the form of Art Deco dressing table sets, often imported from Czechoslovakia. The most popular old styles are still produced there today. They come up at fairs from time to time, but generally speaking the colours of the reproductions are less vibrant, paler shades that lack the richness of the 1920s and 1930s glass.

British glass has been made throughout this century, mainly in the Midlands and Scotland. If you're attracted to this collecting area, but not sure where to start, you need to find out about the main methods of production, which will give you a guide to quality and an idea of value. There were talented makers in the UK producing strongly coloured and textured art glass. Especially collectable are the large bowls and vases. The features to look for are deep colours and bold designs in both moulded and blown glass. An entertaining way to learn about the glass-making techniques is to visit a factory, some of which are listed at the back of the book.

When looking at a piece of glass, ask yourself questions about its origins. See if you can find out which manufacturing method was used. Is it free-blown, blown-moulded, moulded, cast or drawn? Then look at the colour and decoration. Does it look like it was handcrafted or mass produced? Examine the piece to see if there are any maker's marks to give a clue to the date and, finally, look for any repairs or signs of reconstruction. A repair (if it has been well done) needn't deter you from buying a piece that you like – or that you are able to learn from – provided that the price takes account of the condition. As always, a damaged piece will be more difficult to sell on.

CARING FOR GLASS
- Never scrub glass when cleaning it.
- Wash glass in warm soapy water and dry it thoroughly with a soft cloth to avoid staining.
- Store items such as decanters with their stoppers off.
- Empty glassware after use as left liquid can leave a deposit and cause permanent damage.
- Bleaching the inside of a glass can sometimes remove a deposit, but a more serious stain on an expensive piece needs specialist attention.

Paperweights
Veral Marshall

'THEY'RE SO LOVELY TO DUST,' enthuses Veral Marshall, of Burford in Oxfordshire, talking about her extensive collection of antique and modern paperweights.

'My husband's family have been selling paperweights in Burford for many years. For our wedding present, his parents gave me a paperweight dated 1972 from the Strathearn factory in Scotland. It is signed with the Strathearn "S", and as my husband's name is Simon it's very precious to me.

'This started my collecting bug, and for the last twenty-five years it's been hard for me to resist. I've never quite resolved the problem of how we decide what stays in our gallery (*see page 152*) and what comes home with us. It's a matter of negotiating with my husband

By using a magnifying glass, Veral can see any flaws – or perfect details – in her large collection of paperweights.

and mother-in-law. I often think that I'll just keep something at home for a while and then sell it on – but once I've got used to looking at it all the time, I don't want to let it go.

'It's really a joint collection with my husband, and nowadays he and I vie over which of us is the most knowledgeable. My mother-in-law says we're the country's leading experts (there aren't *that* many paperweight experts).

'I love paperweights because they are so very tactile – they're made to be handled. I would never hide them away in a glass cabinet, even though some of them are very valuable. We display them on two tables in the sitting room.

'Colours that fascinate and superb workmanship are the marks of a good paperweight, antique or modern. Although I don't buy for investment purposes, like most collectors I like my money to be spent on something that's going to at least retain its value and probably appreciate.

'Then there's the excitement of the search, which is motivated by the desire to build the best collection one can afford and find. I think that the best collectors are those who have certain paperweights of sentimental value, but who are also constantly improving the quality of their collection. After all, only the very rich can buy everything they find. We've got a French pansy weight from 1850 that we've sold three times. People have bought it, kept it for a few years and then, when they've had the money available, they've traded it in for something else they've wanted more. That's quite a good way for people to collect.

'I often find when I'm handling an antique weight that I'm wondering about its previous owners. I think how lovely it must have looked on a lady's desk; or imagine a Victorian tycoon putting it down when ordering his papers.'

Modern paperweights by the finest makers can be a worthwhile investment. This Perthshire paperweight was made in 1998 and would cost a collector around £98.

COLLECTING PAPERWEIGHTS

The first glass paperweights were made in Venice and Bohemia in the early 1840s, but the French works at Baccarat, Clichy and Saint Louis mastered the technique. Their paperweights from 1846 to 1865, during what's known as the 'golden age', are considered to be the best by collectors. They are usually only found through specialist dealers and can cost from hundreds to many thousands of pounds.

Abstract paperweights aren't considered to have the same technical brilliance as the *millefiori* or lampwork designs. Lampwork is a hand blown figurative design encased in glass. *Millefiori*, which translates as 'a thousand flowers', are small rods of glass cut off and arranged in patterns, then encased in clear glass.

You don't have to pay a lot for an attractive paperweight. Modern ones start from under £10, but these aren't particularly collectable. Collectors pay for rarity, complexity and quality. Some modern weights cost from £50 up to several thousand pounds for the best. There are still various paperweight makers worldwide, but the ones made at Saint Louis and Baccarat, in France, and Perthshire, in Scotland, are superb.

It is difficult for a novice buyer to recognise an antique weight, as the colours don't fade and few were signed or dated. If you're considering spending a lot of money it is always best to go to a reputable dealer.

CHAPTER TWO

Glitter and Gladrags

Clothes and Accessories

Clothes and accessories reflect social convention more than any other kind of collectable. Even a piece of jewellery can reveal a lot about a person, when they lived, what their tastes were and what they could afford to spend on luxuries – all this becomes apparent by looking at how or when it was worn.

COLLECTOR'S TIP

'Find out as much as you can by reading, visiting museums and talking to specialist dealers.'

ANN LOUISE LUTHI

When you look at very old clothes, from the nineteenth century or earlier, what first strikes the eye is how tiny they look. You wonder how a grown woman managed to squeeze into the minute slippers, or fasten the 18-inch (46-cm) waistband. A woman's shape also appears to have changed with the fashions – aided by a daunting array of stays, corsets, liberty bodices and bras. Men's clothes evolved too, though more subtly, from the stiff-collared shirts and waistcoats, obligatory in the early twentieth century, to the soft, loose, casuals worn today.

Although many of us still dress in a similar way to each other, there's a feeling today of being able to move beyond limitations of class or gender. And however modern we might feel, most of us have a few old treasures – perhaps a dress, the odd brooch, a hat or jacket – which we'll happily wear on appropriate occasions. Some collectors, however, take it a step further. They might store and display very old costumes, too delicate and precious to be worn, or only wear clothes from a bygone age. These collectors would never be seen buying clothes in an ordinary high street shop.

TWENTIETH-CENTURY CHIC

During the 1930s and the wartime years, when money was tight and there wasn't a lot in the shops, girls stayed home on Friday nights to set their hair and to sew a new collar or buttons on an old frock, thereby giving it a new lease of life. You sometimes find these 'collar and cuff' sets in second-hand markets, and seeing them immediately conjures up the era of dance bands and ration books. You might also come across two or three matching diamante clips. These aren't earrings or brooches as you first might think, but decorations to change a neckline, making a plain day dress more suitable for evening wear. These sorts of collectables don't cost a fortune, but can become part of an interesting collection.

Personal items – clothes, accessories, cosmetics and jewellery – give a collector enormous scope. Some people are drawn to a particular era and their collection extends into household goods or music. Others like to follow a thread and explore the century's fashions or history through one type of garment.

'So much love and work has gone into the textiles and clothes you find in my shop; it's really a celebration of women,' says collector and dealer Pat Oldman, whose shop, Echoes, could be mistaken for a museum. Over eleven years her emporium has grown into a valuable resource for anyone interested in crafts or fashion – historians, collectors, designers or theatre companies.

'In the past, a lot of the items I've acquired would have been burned or thrown away, so I see myself as a preserver of beautiful things. In a lot of ways, you're always treading in the dark when it comes to value, because so many unique things turn up. I've learned not to be put off by other people's ignorance about the worth of something.'

Before spending a lot, collectors need to be able to recognise the designs of each era, and to tell the difference between an original and a copy. Sometimes, it's simply a matter of looking at style or a label. An experienced collector will know about the feel of materials, manufacturing techniques used at certain times and design features that are right for an era.

You won't have to pay a lot to start a collection; there are plenty of clothes, jewellery and accessories around. Once you develop a taste for quality items, specialist dealers are the place to go, although they can be more expensive. You can hunt around at markets and charity shops, but this takes time and you might never come across what you're looking for.

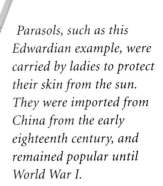

Parasols, such as this Edwardian example, were carried by ladies to protect their skin from the sun. They were imported from China from the early eighteenth century, and remained popular until World War I.

WOMEN'S CLOTHES

Most very old costumes are in established collections, and their owners wouldn't dream of wearing them. But it's not unusual to find people copying the styles to wear at smart costume parties. You can see some of the finest originals on view at various museums, such as the Museum of Costume in Bath or the Victoria and Albert Museum in London. But Victorian clothes turn up regularly at auction house textile sales or through specialist dealers around the country.

'I believe everything should be wearable,' says Pat Oldman. 'After twenty years I'm quite an expert. I know if something's going to drop to bits, even if it looks stunning on the hanger. One sale I went to had Chanel, Worth, all the top names, and I saw someone pay about £800 for a dress that I knew would disintegrate if it was worn.'

Age isn't necessarily an indicator of value. Clothes made in recent decades can be valuable, but quality, design and colour become more important. The fabric should be in good condition. A collector would also judge the general appeal of a dress. In particular, look under the arms for staining – this is where dresses tend to 'go' first. Also, check the hems to see how they've been finished and whether the dress or skirt has ever been altered or shortened.

As time went by, people would adapt clothes to fit their changing figure, or cut them off as hemlines got shorter. The 'new look' fashions of the late 1940s were particularly susceptible to alterations. Christian Dior pioneered a style of clothing that was completely different to anything the world of fashion had previously seen, featuring pencil thin skirts that reached down to the mid-calf, or full circle skirts that used up far more fabric than would have been acceptable during the war. In the 1960s and 1970s there was a craze for the rich velvets and crepes found in old clothes, which were often shortened into minis.

The clothes that are most sought after by collectors are those which evoke the glamour of each decade. The best

Dresses made from semi-transparent silk chiffon were fashionable in the late 1920s and 1930s. This 1930s summer dress from Lucy Kravchenko's collection was made to fit a petite figure. It would have been suitable for a tea-dance – worn with a substantial underslip!

1950s CLOTHES
Sparkle Moore

'I'm into the Hollywood glamour image and I wear my collection. I like to be nicely dressed for cocktail parties,' says Sparkle Moore, who started selling period items so that she could buy some more icons from the 1950s.

'My favourite item is Miss Martini who is a cocktail shaker shaped like a pin-up girl in a gold lamé bikini. I bought her in the USA. My collection makes me feel good and it makes people who see it come out smiling. Although the aesthetics of it are very important to me, so is the humour of it.

'It's mostly based on pin-up images represented in fashion, posters and household items. Also, the modern things that I have fit in with the look and feel of the 1950s, which is what I like.

'I think that my fascination comes from growing up with aunts and uncles who were into 1950s glamour and that rock 'n' roll image. People who collect the 1950s collect different types of things. I know some collectors who wouldn't wear the clothes whereas I like dressing up in them for dinner parties, I don't believe in putting things behind glass. I started selling because I'd collected so many things that I had to sell some of them. Before I had the shop I couldn't part with anything!

'You start collecting because you like a certain item. It builds from liking a particular image and then you find more of that particular thing, some of which you don't want and some that you do. For me it's about having pleasing objects around me that I particularly like.'

Fitted bodices and full skirts were a hallmark of 1950s fashion. This satin dress is decorated with flowers made from beads.

quality garments from the 1920s and 1930s tend to be most expensive. They were a radical change from anything that had gone before – tight laced stays were discarded forever and hemlines rose above the ankle for the first time in history. The changing fashion reflected the growing confidence of women, who had done the work of men during World War I, lived a freer lifestyle and now had more opportunity for financial independence than previous generations. The dress styles of the 1920s were straight, loose fitting and relatively casual – ideal for dancing the Charleston or Tango. If you're lucky enough to come across a flapper dress, it might not have a label, but look at the quality of workmanship to see if it's worth the asking price, which would usually reach a three-figure sum.

Over the decade designers learned the skill of cutting fabric on the cross, so a dress would cling to the figure and reveal the shape. Even more shocking – light, translucent chiffons became popular. These were worn with a silky underslip. We still see these glamorous dresses in 1930s films, such as those featuring dancers Fred Astaire and Ginger Rogers.

The styles of the 1920s and 1930s have remained so popular that they've been copied a lot in new materials, both for fancy dress and for the theatre, which is fine if you know what you are buying and the price is comparatively low. You'll hardly ever come across any pre-World War II clothes at car boot or jumble sales these days – people have learned to treasure them in recent decades.

Yet you can still buy some beautiful clothes surprisingly cheaply, especially if you're prepared to put up with a little damage or alteration. Post war styles, with interesting fabrics and designs can cost very little.

If you are not sure of the date of a piece of clothing, first look at the inside seams. Early on in the twentieth century machines didn't sew zig-zags or overlocked edges. You might find them finished with pinking scissors, which produces a jagged edge. The most expensively finished would be hand sewn with neat overlapping stitches to stop the fabric from fraying. The label CC usually sewn into an inside seam was used during World War II and immediately afterwards to denote a 'Utility' garment, made according to strict guidelines which rationed the amount of fabric that could be used.

Whatever your style, a visit to a specialist shop is guaranteed to evoke nostalgia for a time when women paid attention to every detail of their appearance and men admired them for it.

CARING FOR CLOTHES

- Use mothballs and wrapping to guard against moth damage.
- Don't wash old sequins – they turn to jelly.
- Avoid washing crepe as it shrinks. If a dress is extremely dirty, wash it gently then iron it out while wet, stretching it carefully as you go. Iron on the wrong side to avoid shininess.
- Delicate fabrics such as silk should be rolled not folded or hung.
- If you're wrapping in tissue paper, make sure that it is acid free to prevent rotting.

DANCING COSTUMES
Christine Hall

'I use my costumes when I perform, so it's really a working collection,' says journalist and bellydancer Christine Hall. Also known as Allmeh Amiou, Christine has an extraordinary collection of dancing costumes that she has gathered from all over the world.

'I started dancing when I was quite young and I made my first costume. Since then, I've spent my holidays in the Middle East and the Orient. Wherever I've gone I've looked for costumes. It's a good way of getting to know local people.

'I collect dance costumes from North Africa too. The ones that mean a lot were given as presents or made specially for performances. I've danced in night clubs in Tunisia and on a cruise boat in Turkey, so just looking at the costume brings back everything, even the smells of a place and the taste of the food. I also collect the music, drums, dancing sticks, swords, head-dresses and jewellery.

'Bellydancing exists in many different countries and traditions, but the movements are always soft and natural. The skill of a good dancer is that she is able to isolate parts of her body and make them do what she wants. The type of costume that shows the movement best is the 'cabaret' costume – I have several of these. It's the one you'd use to dance in a restaurant. It's a bra, covered in sequins, a hip belt with long strings of glass beads, a wide skirt and lots of jewellery. In Egypt, dancers are legally obliged to keep their tummies covered – so they use a body stocking. In Turkey there's no such rule and some of the costumes can be quite revealing.'

When buying decorated garments, hold them up and shake them. If bits drop off, it's not well made. All theatrical costumes need to be strong, they have to put up with a lot of wear and tear. If you want to take up bellydancing, your first garment should be a rectangular hip scarf with coins or glass beads (there are some mail order suppliers in England).

Christine, also known as Allmeh Amiou, is shown here dancing in a cabaret costume. Women of all ages can enjoy bellydancing – in Egypt many of the top performers are in their fifties.

1960s Fashion

Nicola Lynes

'I MIGHT SELL SOME EVENTUALLY, possibly when I've retired, and can't walk round wearing minis and go-go boots!' So says Nicola Lynes, who collects things from the 1960s, especially from Biba, the fashion and accessory house.

'I've been into the 1960s thing since I was thirteen. Now I've got bright flowers on all my walls, except on the one that's purple. Biba was about feathers, rich dark colours, fringing, nothing plain. All the colours are so luxurious you could melt into them. I love it.

'I hang round with people who collect 1960s stuff, but they usually concentrate on one area. I find it difficult to do this. I've always got my eye open for vintage clothes shops. I *am* out of control but everybody has to have one vice.

'Sometimes I do swaps with people. Once I swapped a Courreges trouser suit for a Biba coat. Since then I've seen the coat in auction house catalogues, which is heartbreaking.

'I'm very fussy now when it comes to Biba, I don't really like the later stuff, the long

Nicola is seen here holding a Biba minidress. Her flat is decorated in 1960s style, and she surrounds herself with clothes, furniture and other objects from that period.

flowy dresses. I like the early 1960s "op-art" dresses, like the ones Twiggy wore.

'I'm definitely one of the more eccentric collectors. My friends and I dress in 1960s clothes, sit on 1960s chairs, use 1960s cutlery, everything is 1960–1970s.

'My husband and I go shopping separately now. He's into the 1960s too. Money doesn't really come into it, but I always look at the condition and I know if someone's asking too much. If I feel they're just taking advantage, I'll leave it.'

COLLECTING 1960s FASHION

The names that dominated the decade were Mary Quant, Biba and Ossie Clark, and these are the most prestigious designers to collect. They produced the clothes that 'mods' wanted to wear. While the rocker girls still favoured stiletto heels and full skirts with large hairdos, the 'mods' looked radically different in small stubby Cuban-heeled shoes, short straight dresses that used geometric designs, and short bobbed hair. Mary Quant designed accessories, shoes and even make-up to complement her clothes.

Biba, which was the brainchild of stylist Barbara Hulanicki, was one of the small boutiques that changed the way people shopped. Affordable clothes were hung on bent wooden hatstands and clients sat on velvet divans. This might not seem extraordinary these days, but it was a new concept at that time.

Nicola describes how she collects: 'If I buy a dress, I'll look for boots to go with it. While searching, I might come across a pair of shoes that I can't resist. Then I'll need a dress to go with the shoes.'

ACCESSORIES AND COSMETICS

The main costume accessory of the nineteenth century was a fan. By the 1890s almost everyone had one. How a woman held it, fluttered it, flirted with it or closed it spoke volumes. These days collectors value fans for the romance they evoke and for their workmanship. Ladies also carried parasols and reticules – small cloth or leather bags, hung from the wrist. Out at a ball, the bag might have held a dance card and a lace handkerchief, but certainly no cosmetics. It wasn't until the 1920s that a lady could use a powder compact in public without risking the loss of her reputation.

Personal habits had changed radically by the 1950s, when the early morning bus ride into town was memorable for its smells – perfume, nail varnish and hair lacquer mixed with tobacco. A few women even went to work in hair-rollers, covered with a headscarf. In the evening, they'd be transformed by their bouffant hairdos, bright lipstick and stiletto heels. This was the time when no outfit was complete without matching gloves, shoes, hat and bag; when women carried a compact, a comb and a hankie everywhere.

Men's outfits seemed dull by comparison, but a wide brimmed trilby might have covered Brylcreemed hair, and a colourful tie would have cheered up a pinstriped suit. Later in the decade, teenage youth culture emerged in drainpipes and thick soled sneakers.

Collectors of accessories tap into the nostalgia and glamour of each era. Vanity cases and cosmetics of any sort – not only compacts, but also lipsticks and old block mascaras – are often in good condition for the price you pay. They're found by rooting around in unexpected places. For top quality items that are expensively decorated or made from precious metals, try visiting auctions or specialist shops.

This type of compact was known as a 'Camera-pak' or 'Superflapjack'. It carried a lipstick (pull the tassel), powder and cigarettes. Imported from Germany and Japan in the 1930s.

LIPSTICKS
Navinder Bhogal

'The first time I wore a lipstick was on my wedding day and I felt wonderful,' recalls Navinder Bhogal, whose collection of lipsticks stood at 1,200 at the last count.

'Before that I wasn't allowed to wear lipstick, it just wasn't acceptable in my family, so now I just go for it. I love the smell of a new lipstick when it's first opened, but mostly it's the colours that attract me. I try to give myself half an hour to get ready in the mornings, then I have time to try different colours. Sometimes I mix them, or rub them off and start again completely. I suppose it's a playful thing to do, like you would with a toy, it's something I do in private. I buy them whenever I see a new colour. They sometimes change them in a very subtle way. You can get ones that taste of fruits now.

'I started my collection when I couldn't decide which of the ten Avon lipsticks to buy and decided to have them all. I can't imagine that I'll ever get tired of lipsticks. I'm not particularly interested in how old they are, and I never think about selling them, I just think they're wonderful.'

Modern lipsticks were introduced in the 1920s. Early ones were smaller than they are today. During the war, women were advised to keep their lipstick containers. Refills were produced in cardboard, to save metal. Swivel tubes were uncommon until the 1960s. Before that they were push-up.

A well-designed case is an attractive feature. Plastic wasn't used extensively until the late 1950s because it tended to be brittle and broke easily, covering a bag with lipstick.

COLLECTOR'S TIP

'Don't store compacts in polythene. The moisture can't evaporate and the mirror will be destroyed.'

JULIETTE EDWARDS

Powder Compacts
Juliette Edwards

'FOR ME, IT'S A WAY OF LOOKING at women's history,' says Juliette Edwards, of Surrey, who collects ladies' powder compacts.

'I started the British Compact Collectors' Society in 1995 when I had been a collector for about seven years. I had been ill, lost both my parents and given up my job. I was feeling lonely and aimless so the club helped me to make new friends and to rediscover the more frivolous, feminine side of my character. It's not that I would want to go back to such a "dressed-up" time as the 1930s or 1950s, but I've always been interested in people and

Juliette is holding a 'party case' by Stratton, identical to the one used by Elizabeth Taylor in the 1950s film Butterfield 8.

what made women of a particular era "tick". As a teacher, I know plenty about historical women, but I'd never thought much about twentieth-century women's social history until I started my research. Sometimes I show the compacts to older people and enjoy the stories that come out when they see them. One woman told me about how her husband brought her some Evening in Paris perfume

The design of this Coty compact, made in the 1930s, is attributed to the company of René Lalique.

back from France during World War II. It was so precious and rare that she decanted it for all her best friends. One of my compacts has a picture of a male singing star on it, whom this lady and her friend recognised as Jack Buchanan. Ideas of glamour have changed since those days – he certainly wouldn't appeal to modern young women.

'A lot of the information about the compacts comes from old magazines and trade journals. I always want to know their age, why they're made of what they're made of, and their social context. There are plenty of people trying to sell overpriced compacts, so I've started looking at costume jewellery, lipsticks and hair ornaments. One of our regional organisers will be broadening the scope of the newsletter with a column on vintage glamour products.

'I have to be sure an item won't go down in price before spending a lot, say on an enamel-on-silver or novelty compact. If it's for investment, I buy examples that everybody wants, like the Kigu flying saucer. They don't contain precious metals or gems, but people buy them for their novelty and style.

'Now I have 600 or so compacts, and the actual collecting has become less important than running the society. We've got about 300 members around the country. We also get together for a national annual convention and then find we've got other things in common.'

COLLECTING POWDER COMPACTS

Art Deco guilloché set in chrome or nickel. These metals were often used in the 1930s.

Before the 1920s, powder compacts were rare. Beauty was supposed to be natural, so cosmetics were hidden in the boudoir. The earliest compacts were imported from France or the USA at the beginning of the century, though there are rare examples from the late nineteenth century.

By the 1930s the glamour industry was booming and women were powdering their noses in public. Then, in the 1960s, disposable containers and compressed powder changed the face of make-up forever.

When buying vintage compacts, look for examples that have style, novelty, and clever mechanisms to prevent the powder spilling out. Seek out names such as Stratton, Vogue and Kigu. Expect to pay £10 upwards from a specialist dealer.

This good quality American compact, in the 'Saddlebag' shape, carried rouge in the lid and powder in the base.

HANDKERCHIEFS
Brenda Mathews

'At charity shops, you might still get them for 15p each,' says Brenda Mathews of Burgess Hill who has over 2,000 of that most humble of items, the handkerchief. 'I started when I was nine and a friend brought me a souvenir crepe hanky from Sussex. The main interest for me is the subject matter rather than the textiles. Collecting has increased my knowledge of geography and history. There are hankies made to commemorate all sorts of events – festivals, coronations and exhibitions. I was inspired to research the stories behind them.

'I find hankies in charity and bric-a-brac shops and people kindly give them to me. Recently someone sent me a lipstick handkerchief, in red cotton with '*pour la rouge*' embroidered in the corner, obviously used before tissues were the thing.

'One of the advantages is that it's a collection that doesn't need dusting and they're not breakable. I just put them in vinyl sleeves so that they don't get grubby or damaged.'

The term 'pocket handkerchief' was first used in the sixteenth century – you often see large, ornate hankies in old portraits. Up to the end of the nineteenth century they were quite a luxury and the ideal gift. A lady with time on her hands could make one, so you find lace and embroidered silk, as well as the commercially produced commemorative hankies. Special ones often cost pounds rather than pence. You might expect to pay between £5 and £50 for older, rarer ones at antique shops. Regimental and royal ones are particularly sought after, but the prices vary a lot depending as much on where you buy as on what the hanky depicts.

Among Brenda's collection is a hanky displaying the World War I song 'Keep the Home Fires Burning' with lyrics by Ivor Novello, one showing the Duchess of York in 1931 and one commemorating the Berlin Olympic Games in 1936.

GENTLEMEN'S ACCESSORIES

When thinking of accessories and jewellery, we naturally think of women's adornments, including hats, make-up and handkerchiefs. But men also have bits and pieces, such as signet rings, cigarette cases, cuff links and hip flasks, which nowadays they normally only wear on special occasions such as weddings.

In the nineteenth century the size of a man's pocket watch and the materials that it was made out of had a deep significance, as Victorian men's ornaments collector Tony Rothwell explains. 'At the end of the last century, the gentry would wear gold, middle classes silver, and working men might have stainless steel. Later, colliers took to carrying silver or gold pocket watches; the bigger the Albert chain the bigger the status. His Lordship didn't need to do that because he'd got no need to show his wealth – so he'd have something small and discreet, but expensive.'

Many of the watches didn't survive. According to Tony Rothwell, this is because 'whenever the price of gold went up, grandad's watch chain went in the melting pot. And these days, too, when the gold price is high things have intrinsic value – they're worth more than sentimental value.'

Although both sexes smoke, most of the accoutrements that go with smoking were designed for and used by men. While smoking itself has become increasingly frowned upon, gold and silver Vestas (cases for matches) and cigarette boxes are much in demand by collectors for the pictures or decoration on them. Pipes, too, are collected for their variety and aesthetic appeal.

'Don't be scared to barter when buying gentlemen's accessories,' says collector Tony Rothwell. Prices for Victorian jewellery have risen steeply in recent times because of a lot of interest from American and Japanese collectors. Gold Vestas have gone from £80 to £250. But, at the end of a day, dealers at a fair will often be prepared to do a deal.

Old cigarette packets (still with cigarettes inside), matches and tobacco tins are modestly priced, but lighters – small ones for the pocket or large 'coffee table' ornaments – are more expensive. The cost will depend on the materials and design, a plain one might be as little as £5, but the largest aquarium lighters ('seascapes' set in resin) can fetch £300 at a big auction. Some of the accessories produced by the tobacco company Dunhill are also highly sought after. Decorative boxes in novelty shapes, long holders and Vestas all reflect the date they were made. Car boot sales and antique shops are the places to look for these.

Pocket watches were popular up until the 1950s. This one is attractive to collectors because of the novelty of the face design.

VICTORIAN MEN'S ORNAMENTS
Tony Rothwell

'I found an engraved silver Vesta case and thought, a man would work for a week to make something like that, and I can buy it for £8,' remembers Tony Rothwell, a former miner of Nottingham who's fascinated with the adornments which went with the way of life of a Victorian gentleman.

'Imagine a big country estate in about 1890, the place where a gentleman would go to shoot. He's there with a double Albert chain pinned to his waistcoat, mother of pearl shirt buttons, a double sovereign case with five sovereigns and five half sovereigns, holding a full hunter gun. And all that at a time when people were getting paid in coppers. Gentlemen had fantastic lives.

'I started collecting when I inherited a gold pocket watch and chain, then a close friend died and left me a silver one. I go to places like Donnington Collectors' Fair. People get to know you and what you like, and you haggle a bit; that's all part of the fun.

'What attracts me are things the gentry would have had, such as a fob watch, a snuff box, a Lucifer (that's a type of cigarette lighter) and a cigarette box. I read all the books and would have liked the lifestyle.

'I take the collection out of the bank occasionally if it's being shown at an exhibition or something, then I'll sit with a whisky or a cup of tea and just play about with the beautiful things they used to make. Then it has to go straight back in.

'I have big photographs of the collection to look at between times and I still get a kick out of knowing that I've got all of them.'

For those thinking of starting a collection of men's ornaments, or who have inherited an engraved pocket watch or signet ring, Tony has the following advice. 'Never take the initials off a piece of jewellery – they tell part of the story. A man didn't just buy for himself, he bought as an investment for his children and grandchildren. That's why he put the initial on.'

When the gentry took to wearing slimmer, decorative watches, working men sported larger silver, gold plate or nickel ones. This small enamelled gentleman's pocket watch was made between 1880 and 1900.

SMOKING MEMORABILIA
Dr Chris Steele

'I started collecting smoking memorabilia to help people give up,' says Dr Chris Steele of Manchester, a GP who does a medical phone-in on ITV's *This Morning* programme every Thursday. He also runs Europe's busiest stop-smoking clinic, which has been going for twenty years.

'I've got two or three display cabinets full, and bits and pieces up on the walls. I was never really a smoker myself; I tried cigars and pipes, but never stuck with them. Once I started work at the clinic, I began to notice items of smoking paraphernalia and picked them up. I use them as talking points. So, an old packet of Passing Cloud or Senior Service cigarettes, from the 1940s, can jog some chap's memory, and he'll say "I started smoking those when I was eleven…". The collection, which includes beautiful tobacco tins with the price 5d on the outside, shows people I'm not "anti" smoking or an "anti" smoker. I'm just there to help them give up smoking if they want to. It helps build the foundation for our relationship.

'I treat large groups; we have about 120 people all of whom want to give up smoking. I bring out the old lighters and packets – I've even got a novelty mahogany dispenser, in the shape of a cabin, where the cigarette appears miraculously on the "roof". These items get them all talking and laughing, and helps to set the atmosphere.

'It's not an enormous collection and I don't know much about them, although some are very attractive. I've picked things up from car boot sales and antique and junk shops. It has got more expensive now, though, so I'm glad I've got enough to suit my purpose.'

Smoking sparked great creativity in the designers of 'glamour' products. Many of these accessories are now classed as decorative arts and are proving to be irresistible to collectors.

Large 'coffee table' lighters were popular in the 1950s when it was seen as good manners to offer your guests a cigarette.

JEWELLERY

Real jewellery, which is made from precious metals and gems, has always been expensive. For centuries, the accumulation of fine jewellery in almost all cultures has been a way of creating and displaying wealth, and it's still impossible to collect jewellery without investing substantial sums of money.

It used to be only the well-to-do families who could afford jewellery. Then, in the nineteenth century, mass produced adornments became available in a variety of interesting materials. Pieces were mounted in base metals and decorated with semi-precious stones, coloured glass, shells and even pebbles. A lot of items were made up to mimic real pieces, such as pearl necklaces and diamond brooches. By the end of the century, there was something within the price range of almost everybody. For the first time, working women were growing used to the freedom of having a bit of money to spend, and were able to buy jewellery for themselves – even silver was no longer totally out of reach.

The striking difference between jewellery in the nineteenth and the twentieth centuries is that later designers discovered new ways of using inexpensive materials to produce what we now call 'costume jewellery'. Bold and fashionable styles were developed, which didn't even pretend to be the real thing, but were bought to match an outfit. Costume jewellery gained respectability in the 1960s because some of the most chic dressers, notably Coco Chanel and Jackie Kennedy, were unashamed to wear it.

In the 1930s, a Bakelite brooch would have cost little, but these days a collector would pay a lot for the elegant Art Deco styling. Older isn't necessarily better, or more expensive, in this field. It might not be wise to collect costume jewellery as an investment, because the intrinsic value of the materials isn't that great and fashions change. A collector needs to be skilled at spotting a valuable piece and only experience will help him or her to recognise quality.

If a piece of costume jewellery is quite rare, and it is skilfully crafted by a top designer in a fashionable style of the time, then it could be fairly pricey. A serious collector wouldn't flinch at

Jewellery is subject to fashion. These earings from Ann Louise Luthi's collection (see pages 46–7) are made from hair, which was a popular material in the nineteenth century.

paying £100 for a bit of plastic that cost less than 10 shillings when it was made. Happily there are many sources – markets, charity shops, small auctions – where bargains are still to be found.

Diamanté clips such as this were used by women during World War II to change the neckline of a dress.

The back of a piece of jewellery will often hold a clue as to its age. If it has a 'roll over' pin then it must date from after World War II, as this type of fastener was only introduced then. Careful scrutiny can also reveal something about a piece's quality – for instance, better quality brooches often had a loop for a safety chain. When valuing a piece you should also look at the quality of the workmanship – is the piece well finished?

Most costume jewellery wasn't marked. The more expensive pieces were sometimes stamped on the back with a name. One such example is the name Miracle, which was added to pieces made by the Birmingham firm Hill & Co.

Collecting 'real' jewellery is also a matter of becoming practised at spotting quality work. Searching for hallmarks is one of those skills, but not all gold or silver has been hallmarked. With a bit of experience a collector will learn to recognise real gold by its feel. Generally, look at catches and clasps and the way something has been put together. Also, study the differences between real and fake precious stones – many 'diamond' rings and 'pearl' necklaces on the market are impostors.

Collectors' Lot presenter Jethro Marles has worked with fine jewellery for twenty years, time enough to have developed his own taste. 'I like things that have been handcrafted. Take a diamond engagement ring, for instance. If I come across one with a handmade setting – hand-carved, handworked – it takes on a different feeling. It has the energy of the individual who made it, that's basically what I like. I go for individual organic pieces. I especially like the Arts and Crafts pieces from the end of the nineteenth century.'

Whatever the style they are attracted to, flashy or subdued, neat or bold, Victorian or modern, a collector will need to gain knowledge by handling pieces and taking opportunities to look at them closely. One way of doing this is by joining a club and talking to fellow collectors. There is also a myriad of specialist books, which cover the whole range of this huge subject.

CARING FOR JEWELLERY

• A clumsy repair will affect the value of a piece. Ask a jeweller's advice.

• Some silver turns grey with age, but many collectors like the character of it.

• Often, semi-precious and paste stones were backed with foil to make them more shiny. These can be difficult to clean and mustn't be put in water. Try using a dry or damp toothbrush to loosen the dirt.

Sentimental Jewellery

Ann Louise Luthi

Ann is seen here with some of her 200 pieces of hair jewellery. She would like to see her collection in a museum one day.

'WORD GOT ROUND that there was a crazy woman buying jewellery made of human hair. Very soon, every dealer in London knew about me,' says Ann Louise Luthi. She collects something that most people don't want.

'My collection started around ten years ago when my mother-in-law died and left me some money. I bought a piece of mourning jewellery in her memory and became interested in buying more. I soon discovered that the dealers who sold mourning jewellery also had jewellery made of hair, which no one seemed to be buying. Hair is regarded as distasteful by many people and dealers will

During the nineteenth century hair was used as a material in its own right, to make bracelets, rings, earrings, necklaces, watch chains and brooches.

often remove the hair in order to make a piece of jewellery more saleable.

'There is very little hair jewellery in museum collections and it is not highly regarded by the experts. That is part of the challenge, and also the pleasure of collecting. I like saving pieces that might otherwise not survive.

'For me, the aesthetic and historical are both important. I only buy what I find attractive, but many of these pieces also have inscriptions that provide a very poignant insight into the lives of the families who first owned them. I have one piece which commemorates the deaths of a father and son who were drowned together when their ship sank.

'I usually wear ordinary costume jewellery, but I sometimes wear pieces from my collection for special occasions. Hair is quite vulnerable so I have to be careful not to get caught in the rain or to do the washing up while I'm wearing it.

'I'm probably not a typical collector; I don't have any other collections. My husband never threw anything out – he was much more of a magpie than I am. But collecting can become an obsession and I sometimes find myself economising so that I can buy more pieces.

'It's becoming more difficult to find things and prices are going up. I don't think my collection will ever be complete, but I may one day give it all to a museum. Provided I can find a museum that would want it.'

COLLECTING SENTIMENTAL JEWELLERY

The hoop in this earring is fashioned from hair.

Hair was used for love tokens as well as for mourning jewellery. Before the days of photographs, when portraits were expensive, hair was a personal gift that did not deteriorate in time. In the eighteenth century engaged couples might give each other hair to be worn as a bracelet and a mourning ring was a way of remembering a loved one who had died.

In the nineteenth century, hair was increasingly used as a material in its own right to make jewellery that was not necessarily connected with a particular person. At this time other natural materials were also popular. Coral, jet, ivory, pebbles, fossils and horsehair were all used in jewellery.

There is still a lot of moderately priced hair jewellery around, but good quality items cost more.

Cross, beads and earrings all made of hair.

CHAPTER THREE

Stargazing

Showbusiness Memorabilia

Actors, musicians, performers and entertainers lift the human spirit by offering an escape from the mundane into a world of glamour and romance. In recent years stars have received an unprecedented amount of coverage, and an industry has grown up marketing related memorabilia.

In the nineteenth century and earlier, talented players and musicians could make a name for themselves by touring regional theatres. The violinist Paganini, for example, enjoyed superstar status – women fans threw their clothes at him to attract attention. Others, Edward and Charles Keen, for instance, were famous for their portrayal of Shakespearean characters. Then in the mid-nineteenth century, the music hall tradition grew from 'glee' clubs and artists emerged from the back rows of pubs to entertain wider audiences.

The stars of silent movies enjoyed a celebrity status previously unheard of. However, the size of audience that flocked to see Charlie Chaplin or Ivor Novello was small when compared to the millions that tune in today to watch the most popular television programmes, and the millions more who buy the albums of their favourite rock stars. Through the publicity that they attract, stars become so well known that fans sometimes begin to think of them as close friends or even extensions of the family. Then, as time goes by, we share nostalgia for what they represent.

ROGER MOORE
Mike Wilson

'It's pure escapism: car chases, exotic locations, wonderful dry humour and predictable plots,' says London graphic designer Mike Wilson, who has devoted a room to Roger Moore.

'Roger was a kind of role model in my teenage years. He always played such suave characters, the epitome of the heroic English gentleman. I've been a fan since 1971 when he was Lord Brett Sinclair in *The Persuaders*, co-starring with Tony Curtis. His Bond was more tongue-in-cheek than Connery's. I've heard he's fun to work with and likes a relaxed light-hearted atmosphere. He knows about my collection and it's my ambition to meet him because I feel like he's an old friend.

'The collection started back in 1979. I'd just seen *Moonraker* and bought a poster for around £5 – it's worth hundreds now. I like the challenge of finding something new and different. I get a lot from specialist shops in London's West End and also have friends in other countries who send me bits and pieces. I have theatre programmes from the 1940s and a knitting pattern he modelled before he became famous.

'I'll always collect, but I do other things too. It can be a social thing – it's so nice to be in the company of people who have the same interest. Part of the fun is the chase. I just hope I can afford it when I find it!'

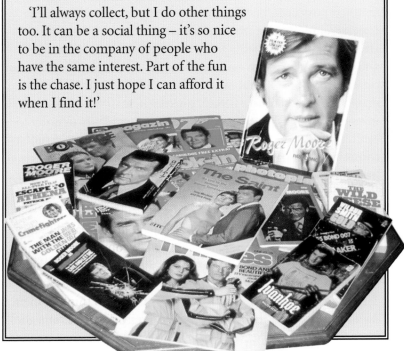

A fraction of Mike's enormous collection of Roger Moore memorabilia, which includes magazines and newspapers. They have come from the USA, Germany, the Netherlands, France, Spain, Italy and Japan.

FILM MEMORABILIA

In the 1920s, music halls and theatres gave way to cinemas as the most popular venues for entertainment. The low cost of tickets meant that more people were able to afford the pleasure of a good night out at the flicks. Hollywood movie stars offered an escape from the day to day struggles of the 1920s and 1930s. Their glamour helped people through the Depression, leaving them with strong images of how it was possible to manage and thrive elsewhere. People adored them. Studios couldn't recruit enough of the starlets who might follow in the footsteps of such greats as Greta Garbo, Dorothy Lamour and Marlene Dietrich. It was still a novelty to see images that looked so real you could almost touch them. What the stars said and did mattered to millions.

The word 'fan' comes from 'fanatic' – someone who is an enthusiastic supporter. The Americans first used it in 1889 to describe sports followers. By the 1930s it was used colloquially in England and applied as much to those who admired entertainers as to sportsmen and women.

There was no shortage of fans. Paramount, MGM, Universal Artists, RKO, Warner Brothers and 20th Century Fox in the USA, and J. Arthur Rank in Britain, all had publicity departments that were keen to exploit the public's interest in their stars by producing souvenirs. Until the 1950s, these were mostly pictures of one sort or another: postcards, photographs and prints. All of the studios worked hand in glove with private companies, encouraging their stars to promote everything from knitting patterns to jewellery. Tobacco manufacturers put picture cards of stars inside packets of cigarettes. The Lux Toilet Soap Movie Club had its own fan magazines. Studios were fiercely possessive and protective of their investments, however, and would censor all publicity in order to avoid unseemly scandals. Newspapers and magazines that didn't comply with the studio's regulations soon found that the source of their information had dried up.

Merchandise produced for filmgoers was gradually extended, particularly during the 1960s. These days, it's common to find a whole range of consumer products riding on the back of a new film, particularly if it has appeal for children. The list of Disney and Warner Brothers merchandise is so extensive that specialist shops have been opened over the past decade to cater for the growing demand. So mass marketing has made it feasible for people to have the image or object they want at an affordable price and without having to go too far out of their way to get it.

Cheap, mass-produced plastic toys often become collectors' items. This plastic figure is of the Wookie Chewbacca from the blockbuster Star Wars.

COLLECTING FILM MEMORABILIA

The continuing popularity of a character or genre, together with the quality and scarcity of the item will determine how much a collector might have to pay for film merchandise.

A film doesn't have to be old to attract the attention of collectors, though the 1920s silent movies always hold a special interest. Some genres – notably science fiction – become collectable as soon as a successful film is released. Generally, however, as far as recently made items are concerned, it could be a long time before the resale value exceeds the original retail price of souvenirs, and it isn't uncommon for things to fall in value in the shorter term.

Some goods are sold as 'limited editions', particularly toys and specially made pottery, possibly in the hope that collectors will see them as an investment. There are plenty of these items around at present, however, so buying for this reason is quite a gamble. As a general rule, film memorabilia associated with characters that have stood the test of time, such as James Bond, the Star Trek crew and King Kong, continues to be in demand.

The most expensive vintage film memorabilia is in a different league to the recently manufactured souvenirs or reproductions. Auction house sales include items such as original film posters, contemporary toys, props used on the sets, costumes and personal possessions of stars, or the original artwork from an animated film. These sorts of things might have belonged to someone who worked on the film, so it's unlikely that they'll be found while you are browsing around a market. The prices are not always sky high, in fact dealers often buy at auctions such as these, but it only takes two people to want the same thing to push the price up. And there'll be a commission to pay on top, usually 10 to 15 per cent.

Specialist film or entertainment memorabilia shops, where the dealer is a fellow enthusiast, are a good place to browse and accumulate knowledge. They'll be more expensive than markets, but there is more chance of success if you're looking for something in particular. These shops thrive in most major cities, so they shouldn't be so difficult to find in the telephone book.

Collectors' Film Conventions are also an excellent place to foster an interest and to see what's available. You'll find them listed in film magazines such as *Empire*. The price is often very competitive, reflecting the real demand for certain items.

Car boot sales are always fun, and that's where the bargains are. They're always good for reproductions and you might even spot an original once you've learned to recognise them.

COLLECTOR'S TIP

'Be aware of fluctuations in collectors' markets, which mean prices may drop temporarily.'

DAVID MILES

James Bond

Nick Bennett

'I'M A REGULAR GUY with a bit of a fascination,' says James Bond collector Nick Bennett, who has always cherished the toys he remembers from his childhood.

'I think of collecting as a disease I've contracted. I was always a bit of a hoarder as a child. I'd never throw anything away, just in case I could use it later in life.

'Bond is the focus of my collection, and I'm mostly interested in the toys, books and other odd items. At first any Bond merchandise would do, but it's become important to have things in good condition, with the packaging intact if possible. My business now is selling toys, which follows on from collecting them.

'I enjoy going to the US occasionally to meet other collectors. I have some collecting friends who live locally too. For me, another part of it is the history; I like finding out about the companies who made the items.

Nick is seen here in his office, one corner of which is filled by his Bond collection. He enjoys the view from his desk as he runs his mail order business.

'I don't try to live the life of Bond, though I can see the appeal – fame, fortune, women, drink, excitement. On reflection, maybe the attraction is a world domination thing and I should be collecting the baddies instead.

'I do exhibitions, so I'm buying with that in mind at present. I've enjoyed collecting over the years, but one of the points has been that one day I'll enjoy selling it too. I do get rid of things these days, so I like to think that I have my "disease" under control.'

COLLECTING JAMES BOND

Dr No (1961) was the first Bond film. Its huge success was unexpected, and no merchandise had been prepared. Collectors might find a poster or other publicity prints (at around £500 in good condition) in a specialist shop.

Early Bond toys were dolls of James and Odd-Job. They were brought out after *Goldfinger* (1964) was released. Since then, every film has spawned toys, dolls, clothes and 007 images on just about everything.

Bond films were among the earliest to have associated merchandise. The quality was consistently good and the appeal of 007 lives on, which is why prices have continued to rise.

Original posters and toys, 007 clothes, board games and novelty items are all collectable. There were so many made in the 1970s and 1980s that the price is unlikely to be prohibitive. The earlier, rarer items command the highest prices. Props and costumes from the film come up for sale occasionally, usually costing several hundred pounds.

Danbury Mint limited edition Aston Martin DB5 (1997) and Gilbert figure (1965).

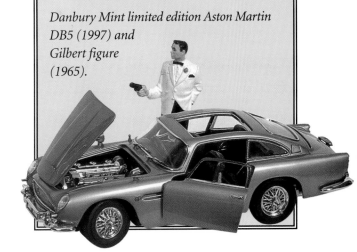

FILM MERCHANDISE

Film companies first realised the gains to be made by linking films with accompanying memorabilia in the 1960s. Not surprisingly, the dolls, vehicles, models and games that date from that time are all attractive additions to a collection. Collectors can expect to pay between £10 and £25 for a recently made Corgi Bond toy. The rare 1960s die-cast Aston Martin will cost closer to £150 these days. Quality merchandise from the 1970s also commands high prices – models from *Moonraker* (1979), such as a helicopter in its original box, cost around £50–£60 now.

Today's film merchandise fits a standard profile: the T-shirt, baseball cap and mug are guaranteed to be produced. A few items, however, will capture the public's imagination. Quality goods that have a particular relevance to the film, such as early models of *Star Trek*'s Starship *Enterprise* or a *Star Wars* character doll, are the products that are likely to interest tomorrow's collectors. Toy companies pay a licence fee to use a film character's name. These can cost huge sums of money, especially for a film aimed at children. The cost to the manufacturer is passed on in the purchase price.

This toy of James Bond has the British secret agent dressed in his scuba gear to fight his enemy in the film Thunderball *and make his getaway in his multi-gadgeted speed boat.*

Posters are one of the most popular kinds of film merchandise – collectors love them for their decorative appeal as much as for the person or landscape that is portrayed. Most attractive are posters with artwork that is typical of its time, with good, strong colours and quality reproduction. Some of the best artists worked in the film industry, drawing stars for publicity pictures and designing posters.

Many posters still cost under £20, and there are plenty of reproductions of the old favourites, which should cost only a few pounds. You'll recognise these because new paper will feel different to the old and the reproductions are often more glossy. Also, the name and date along the bottom are a give-away. They aren't usually sold as originals, so you might find them either folded or rolled. You could be offered a choice of price, say £15 rolled (avoiding the creases) or £11.50 folded.

If you're hoping to buy an original poster of a successful film – with a popular actor and quality artwork – then the price can rocket into hundreds or, very occasionally, even thousands. The fact that most film posters were American has tended to push up the prices in Britain. The condition of a poster is important – creases, folds and damage from nails or glue will all seriously detract from the top price. Some posters were trimmed around the edges, so that they would fit into a particular space – a billboard or site on the London Underground, for example. This would also affect the price considerably.

After World War II, posters for films made at Ealing Studios were imaginatively designed, and now they're among the most sought after. The comedies celebrated British eccentricity and many of the more serious films were creatively made and internationally successful. Posters were printed in most European languages, so you might find several different versions.

When it comes to posters, condition counts for a lot, but don't pass over the opportunity to pick up a special item on account of it. You may get it at a good price *because* it's in poor condition. Then you can sell it on for an equally small amount when you come across a suitably pristine version.

Film characters have been used to sell almost every kind of product, including rubber bands.

POSTER GLOSSARY

Posters are described by studio, location and size: *The Last Emperor*, 1987, Columbia, British one-sheet.

⭐ One-sheet: 41 x 27 in (104 x 69 cm), usually with two horizontal and one vertical fold.

⭐ Three-sheet: 81 x 41 in (206 x 104 cm), printed on two or three sheets to be pasted up on walls.

⭐ Half-sheet: 22 x 28 in (56 x 71 cm).

⭐ Inserts: 36 x 14 in (91 x 36 cm).

⭐ Lobby cards: set of eight publicity cards.

Marilyn Monroe

Michelle Morgan

'WHAT STILL INTRIGUES ME is how anyone could have thought she was dumb when she had so much wit and intelligence,' says Michelle Morgan, who collects books and other memorabilia of the 1950s screen goddess Marilyn Monroe.

'I was on holiday when I first discovered Marilyn. I became fascinated, maybe because she was so pretty and I was fifteen and not at all glamorous. I read a book and bought a few postcards. I didn't set out to collect, but now I've got about 140 books on her.

Michelle is pictured holding a copy of her book Marilyn's Addresses. *The model of Marilyn's house, which was made for Michelle by her father, is displayed on a shelf above her bed. Books, toys and posters also form part of her collection.*

'I even went to the States to visit places where she'd been and turned the journey into a book called *Marilyn's Addresses*. I run a club and, through this, I got a rare interview with her first husband, James Dougherty. Half the people I know, I've met through Marilyn.

Marilyn Monroe – An American Beauty Classic is one of a set of six dolls based on the actress that have been manufactured especially for collectors in the 1990s. Each of the dolls is wearing a different outfit.

'I'm interested in women who've come from nowhere and made something of their lives, like Marilyn. She wanted so much to be taken seriously, it breaks my heart to think of it. It's sad that she died so young. She'd be in her seventies now, with grandchildren running around.

'I'd love to own something she wore, I've seen a few things, but they're so expensive you'd have to keep them in the bank. The most important thing to me is a model of her house that my dad made for me. Like a lot of my collection, it's worth nothing to other people, only to me.'

COLLECTING MARILYN MONROE

Marilyn Monroe was born Norma Jean Baker in 1926. She had already built up a successful modelling career when her acting talent was acknowledged in *All About Eve* (1950), and her greatest films include *Gentlemen Prefer Blondes* (1953), *The Seven-Year Itch* (1955), *Bus Stop* (1956), *Some Like It Hot* (1959) and *The Misfits* (1960). Her huge success made her hot property, but aroused strong feelings, both at work and at home.

She set up her own production company to make *The Prince and the Showgirl*, co-starring Lawrence Olivier, although it is rumoured that the two didn't get on.

Years after her untimely death in 1962, the details of which are still steeped in controversy, her legend shows no sign of waning.

This figurine is based on a famous scene from the film Gentlemen Prefer Blondes *(1953).*

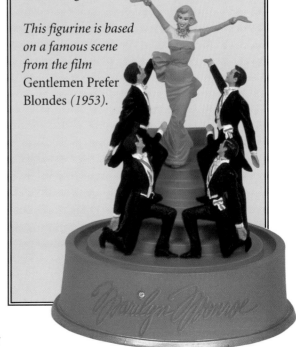

PRINTED FILM EPHEMERA

Printed pictures and signed autographs of major stars command big money. This rule not only applies to the 'Hollywood Greats', but also to the battery of British stars who made films at Ealing, Pinewood or Elstree studios. Publicity material such as this was printed in great numbers, however, so it needs to have something special about it to be worth more than a few pounds. Pictures and postcards should date from the time a film was released. Collectors should bear in mind that there are many reproductions, which are fine if they are priced accordingly.

Pictures of early silent movie stars, such as Douglas Fairbanks and Mary Pickford, are more difficult to find because there were fewer published – the studios had yet to realise how strong the link was between advance publicity and box office receipts. This rarity factor will probably be reflected in the price.

A collector will pay a lot for a genuine autograph. During the 1930s, signed photographs of stars were sent out to fans who wrote to the studios. These days some of them are valuable, but prices vary dramatically, depending on the current popularity of the star, the date and the rarity of the signature – some stars put a great deal of time and energy into promoting themselves, while others were practically recluses.

If you're not sure whether a signature is authentic, don't be afraid to ask for confirmation before paying a lot of money. You can demand a written receipt. Then, if the signature turns out to be a forgery, you'll be able to get your money back under the Sale of Goods Act, 1979.

Publishing houses first developed magazines for film fans in the 1920s. They were compatible with the studios' desire for publicity. It's not hard to imagine that 'official' fan clubs were set up by press departments asking an avid fan to be its 'secretary' as a means of promoting movies and actors.

Film magazines of the 1930s, 1940s and 1950s are rich pickings for collectors who want to get an insight into the lifestyles of their favourite stars – even if they are being shown a thoroughly sanitised view. *British Screen*, *Film Fiction* or *Screen Pictorial* are all magazines that are collectable now. Most of them will cost just a few pounds, but first editions are more expensive, usually they sell for between £25 and £50.

Of course, films weren't the only entertainment in the 1920s and 1930s. Hungry for publicity, radio and an emerging record industry were also trying to push their stars.

IVOR NOVELLO
Malcolm Dickie

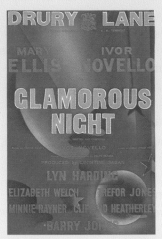

'It all began with my grandfather who had some Ivor Novello music in his piano stool. I noticed a piece of sheet music at my grandfather's called 'Keep the Home Fires Burning' and asked him to play it. Novello wrote the lyrics in 1914 for people going off to war. I thought it was full of spirit so I took it to school and sang it an end-of-term concert.' Malcolm Dickie of Essex, now collects everything to do with the actor, composer, director and producer, Ivor Novello (1893–1951). Malcolm also is a co-founder of the Ivor Novello Society and sings the music from his shows.

'I've got a lot of sheet music, including some original manuscripts from shows. I find them at ephemera fairs and even car boot sales. At a sale some years ago, a man had a quantity of music, first-night programmes, photographs and cards. He just wanted to get rid of them and only charged a few pounds for the lot. I don't find as much as I did twenty years ago, but sometimes I'm lucky. I found a rare 78 RPM record of 'Ghosts' from the 1937 musical *Crest of the Wave* – only two are known to exist.

'There's no catalogue to go by; no fixed prices. One postcard and autograph shop offered me some signed postcards for £75 each. But I declined because you can still pick them up for £15–£25 at a postcard fair.

'A crocodile briefcase, made by Aspreys for Ivor Novello in the 1930s was left to me in the will of a woman I became friends with. Whenever she came into Harrods, where I once worked, we'd talk about Ivor Novello. The briefcase is my most treasured possession.

'When I sing the songs – 'We'll Gather Lilacs', 'Love is My Reason', 'Waltz of My Heart' – I feel his presence, as though he sings through me. He was an all round genius of his time.'

Although he is best known for his musicals such as Glamorous Night *(above left), Ivor Novello was also a successful film star. Publicity shots, such as this signed photograph (below), would have been available from his agent or the company he was working with at the time.*

From a photograph by Cecil Beaton.

ROCK AND POP

Rock and pop collectables are closely related to film memorabilia so, as you would expect, some of the same criteria apply. The obvious treasures – such as a guitar that belonged to Elvis Presley – are rare and unlikely to come up very often. For that reason, there will be a great demand and prices will soar. Contracts, lyrics or letters in the artist's own hand and autographs are all highly valued, particularly if they date to a time before the person had reached the peak of a successful career. But before paying a lot for something like this, it is important to check the provenance. Signatures, in particular, are notoriously easy to copy, and some bands had a habit of getting the back stage staff to sign autographs on their behalf, so this is an area where experience and knowledge count.

Since Bob Geldof organised the Live-Aid famine relief concert in October 1984, rock musicians have been particularly linked with good causes. Their personal possessions and stage costumes are regularly donated to charity auctions. That means collectors have the opportunity to acquire items that wouldn't otherwise have come up for sale. Things that mark particularly important events in a career, such as the guitar that John Lennon used to record The Beatles' first hit 'Love Me Do', are the most prized, but any celebrity's belongings are treasured. There are also collectors who will buy a fairly ordinary item for more than it's worth because of who owned it. Provenance is important, and can vastly affect the value. This is one of the ways that the market for personal possessions is unpredictable – if some of these items that come up for sale had belonged to anyone else, then they'd be worth comparatively little.

The future value of these personal possessions is uncertain, and will rise or fall with the fortunes of each individual and the fashion. But a lot of fun can be gained from spotting whose success may be long lasting and who will decline into obscurity. Sadly, an early death will turn the memorabilia of cult figures into

The American singer and actress Madonna shot to fame in the mid-1980s with hits that included 'Like a Virgin' and 'Material Girl'. She sold millions of records, so it is unlikely that even limited editions will be valuable for many years to come.

poignant relics. John Lennon, Elvis Presley, Buddy Holly, Jimi Hendrix, Freddie Mercury, Jim Morrison and Marc Bolan are a few of the great talents who hold a special place in people's hearts and whose possessions are treasured.

Unsigned pictures or souvenirs made in large quantities to promote an album, are of little monetary value. There is a steady supply of them at specialist fairs and markets for just a few pounds upwards. Basically, most items of this sort are worth what a collector is willing to pay.

Programmes from pop concerts and revues are also highly collectable. The above example tells of a late night appearance by Cliff Richard.

Concert posters of the 1960s are eminently collectable. People are attracted to the bright colours and psychedelic designs. They have since been imitated but never with quite the same panache. Originals are rare and you can expect to pay around £150 to £200, although prices vary widely depending on condition, design and which band or singer is featured. Many were reprinted from the original plates shortly afterwards, to adorn the walls of young people who saw them as an alternative to paintings. These vary a little in value, but expect to pay around £30 to £50. Particularly sought after are the artists Stanley Mouse and Rick Griffin, who designed posters in San Francisco for the Family Dog Production Company and Bill Graham's Fillmore Hall posters. Recent reproductions taken from the original plates exist and fetch around £15 to £20 each, but the colours vary from the originals.

Posters from today's concerts are not all going to be collectable. If you like it, or if it's been designed by a recognised artist, then it could be worth putting away. Most are printed in vast quantities and many more people are inclined to keep them these days.

By the time the rock 'n' roll industry was well underway, towards the end of the 1960s, promoters had learned a thing or two about producing souvenirs for fans. Go to any rock concert these days and you're bound to find stalls full of official merchandise, not only souvenir programmes, but T-shirts, posters, mugs and so on. One day these may become good investments, but, again, their price will follow the fortunes of the artist. As always, buy for love rather than for money.

Cliff Richard
Shirley Abrey

'I'VE MET HIM RECENTLY,' says Shirley Abrey, a Cliff Richard fan of Hampton, Middlesex. 'I stayed up all night outside Tower Records in Piccadilly until he arrived to do a signing session. I thought there'd be other fans there, but I was on my own until 4am and terrified!

'It all started when I was sixteen. I had just left school and was an apprentice hairdresser. I came back from work one Saturday night and there he was on TV – singing on 'Oh, Boy!' I thought he was the most gorgeous thing. The

Shirley has clocks, photographs of her and Cliff together and of him receiving his knighthood, books, concert programmes, videos and the wig Mike Yarwood wore to impersonate him.

first record I bought had 'Move It' on the A side and 'Schoolboy Crush' on the B side.

I became even more of a fan as the years went by. Now I'm fifty-one, with five grand-children. Whenever there's a concert, one of the family gives me a ticket and the others chip

This double-hearted picture disc, with an image of Cliff in the middle, has 'Two Hearts' on the A side and 'Yesterday, Today, Forever' on the B side.

in to help me buy the discs and T-shirts and so on. I have all the records on CD, tape and LP when possible.

'People think you're off your trolley to be so besotted. That was why I used to run a "meeting house" – that's where you advertise in the paper that you're having a "Cliff" evening and ten or so fans come around to play records, do quizzes and let themselves go. It's quite the done thing, more so than being a member of the fan club. You get a huge mixture of people, all women, although the concerts are also well attended by men.

'My husband, Ken, is sympathetic but he winds me up. He and my son set me up for the TV programme *Beadle's About* by gradually taking bits of my collection out of the house. I thought I was going mad! I've also been on *The Time, The Place* and *Kilroy* with my collection.

'One room at home is dedicated to press cuttings, which are all over the walls. Half of our bedroom – my half – is covered in photographs and posters. My favourite items are a gold brooch with gemstones spelling out Cliff, photographs of Cliff and myself and the programme of a concert called The Event.

COLLECTING CLIFF RICHARD

Cliff Richard, who started life as Harry Webb, was born on 14 October 1940. He first hit the teen scene in 1958, as singer with The Shadows. At first he was an English rival for Elvis Presley, but with his own style.

The way to find records is to pick them up at a record collector's shop or to trawl through car boot sales. It's worth getting friends and relatives to join in the hunt – Shirley's neighbour goes to car boot sales weekly and buys any Cliff Richard records she finds for Shirley, who doesn't mind how many copies she has of a recording.

This EMI picture disc was released in 1984. Rare picture discs date from the 1920s, but were most commonly produced in the 1970s and 1980s before CDs replaced vinyl.

RADIO AND TELEVISION

Radio and television have been an inspiration to collectors. The memories of programmes as diverse as *Muffin the Mule*, *Z-Cars* and *Thunderbirds* live on in collections. Soaps, such as *Crossroads*, also have their fans. But top of the pile has to be the stunning line-up of British comedy shows. They were made to be ephemeral, but successive generations find them a joy to watch. They inspire such loyalty from collectors who can recite lines and catchphrases from memory, as well as mimic characters. They tell us so much about the British sense of humour. *Hancock's Half Hour*, *The Goon Show*, *Dad's Army*, *The Morecambe and Wise Show*, *Monty Python's Flying Circus* and many more have lived on beyond their 'sell by' dates. The memories we have of radio stars are to be found only in photographs and audio tapes, but some of the TV shows from the 1970s onwards inspired board games, books, annuals or toys. Look out for these in charity shops, collectors' toy fairs, car boot sales and markets.

MORECAMBE AND WISE
David Miles

David Miles has painstakingly built his extensive collection of Morecambe and Wise memorabilia over many years. He's the first to admit that he owes part of his success to the help he's had from Eric Morecambe's son, Gary. In particular, Gary has been able to assure David that clothes and other items in the collection actually belonged to his father. Provenance is all important in a collection of this sort.

David's Lancashire home is filled with a variety of bills and photographs of the comedian Eric Morecambe.

'You have to spend time looking in car boot sales and shops that sell postcards or bits and bobs, and at specialist collectors fairs,' says David. 'In fact you always have to have your collection in mind wherever you go.'

Perhaps because David moved to Morecambe in Lancashire, where Eric Morecambe once lived, he has been lucky in finding treasures – such as a signed copy of a book of scripts, which he bought in mint condition for £5 in a local shop.

DAD'S ARMY
Tony Pritchard

'The humour is timeless. It's not jokes so much as the funny situations,' says *Dad's Army* collector, Tony Pritchard of Gloucestershire.

'I like all sorts of comedy programmes, including radio shows from the 1960s, such as *The Navy Lark* and *The Clitheroe Kid*. I had over fifty shows of *Dad's Army*, so I set out to find out about the rest. It's brilliant situation comedy, all the characters developed their own humour. It doesn't seem to date in the same way other shows do.

'As part of the research for a book I set out on a trail to find the locations where they were filmed. That really did get addictive, we made it our holiday and it took us to places we'd never have found otherwise. I still watch the programmes a few times a week. I do quite a bit of work with the Dad's Army Appreciation Society – artwork and articles, it takes quite a lot of time, but it's such pleasure. I admit it gets a bit cliquey at conventions, when you hear everyone coming out with their favourite phrases and quips from the show, but no, we don't dress up.'

Dad's Army was first shown on BBC1 thirty years ago and ran for nine years. The current Dad's Army Appreciation Society organises conventions, outings and showings of rare films. *Dad's Army* stars were quite elderly when the series was filmed. Arthur Lowe died in 1982, and John le Mesurier in 1983. Collectors cherish tapes of the programme (five have apparently been lost) signed pictures and autographs, items made as souvenirs of the television programmes and the 1975 stage show – mugs, badges and posters – a board game, and books written by members of the cast and the scriptwriters. An official souvenir costing 20p in 1973 might sell for around £25–£30 at this year's Dad's Army Appreciation Society convention.

This helmet belonged to a World War II ambulance driver. Helmets with different letters were worn by others in the home guard. One of the running battles in Dad's Army *was between Captain Mainwaring and the air-raid warden, Hodges.*

CHAPTER FOUR

Pleasure and Play

Leisure Activities

Playtime is a serious business – and never more so than at the turn of the twenty-first century, when sports, leisure pursuits and playthings are enjoyed by the masses and marketed as never before.

COLLECTOR'S TIP

'The meetings organised by collectors clubs are an excellent way to meet people of like mind and to add to your collection by swapping or buying.'

KEITH WILKINSON

Some of the most interesting and desirable toys and leisure goods date from the Victorian and Edwardian periods, although lasting artefacts tend to be associated with the wealthy upper and steadily emerging middle classes. The leisured classes had time to fill and social obligations to meet. Also, their children needed to be educated and there was a growing belief in learning through play. As a result, the leisure industries produced playing cards, puzzles and amusements specially for children. By the turn of the twentieth century, more people were able to afford playthings. Modern manufacturing techniques meant that leisure goods could be mass-produced, so that toys, games and sporting equipment became more widely accessible.

Maybe some of our nostalgia for playthings past comes from a memory of a smaller, more sociable world. Before computer games, television and affordable weekend flights to New York, people lived at a more leisured pace. It was a time when friends met for a game of cards, children played marbles in car-free streets and a new Victory wooden jigsaw puzzle was considered a main Christmas present.

PINBALL MACHINES
Philip Crow

'When I was fourteen, my parents bought me a pinball machine for my birthday.' Now Philip Crow, who lives in North London, has about 220 pinball machines and plans to open a museum capturing the origins and development of pinball machines.

'My passion for pinballs grew with age – and it all started when I saw one in a hotel in Majorca where I was on holiday with my parents as a teenager.

'I was overjoyed to be given one as a birthday present – and discovered I not only loved playing pinball, but also that I could fix the machines.

'At college I acquired three more and then, once I was out earning, the collection took over my parents' house and I had to hire a warehouse as well as my own place to store them. I've got about fifty of them at home.

'They are so much better than video games. They're more physical, and you're very aware of what they're made of: steel, plastic, rubber, metal. I like the colouring, the artwork and the style of the 1950s and 1960s, which they represent.'

Pinballs were part of the post-War teenage cult. These days, for a mid-1960s model, restored, you could pay £500 plus. For a 1950s version, around £1,000. The days when you could pick them up for £25 are gone.

Although they are classed as gaming machines, there is no money to be won playing pinball. Nowadays, most pub owners prefer to install fruit machines, as they are likely to make a greater profit on them. Pinballs came from simple bagatelle games. Then, in the 1930s, the makers started to introduce power. It wasn't until the first power-driven pinball with flippers was introduced, in the US in 1947, that they became widespread. They are pretty well all from the USA.

People collect the advertising literature: a flyer advertising a pinball machine of the 1960s would go for £5 upwards. Some also collect the 'back glass' from machines that have been broken up – these usually depict a theme, such as a film or sporting event, and are typical of their time, in terms of typeface, graphics and colours.

> ### COLLECTOR'S TIP
>
> *'Things that have a wider, international appeal tend to be more expensive to collect. Prices of the same model might vary from country to country.'*

CHEAP TOYS
David and Jane Housham

'We like to collect anything that is connected to the popular culture of its day,' says Jane Housham, who, together with her husband David, collects the sorts of things that cost little when they were new and were *never* expected to be treasured as 'antiques'.

Items in their collection range from Festival of Britain souvenirs to advertising ephemera, to collectables from the Butlins holiday camps, and many other 'kitsch' items. People must love them at Christmas, when they are keen to give a home to the cracker toys that no-one else wants, the cruder and more garish the better.

'It's lovely when you pick something up that's survived when it wasn't expected to. We find that toys are great ciphers for things that were happening in the adult world. You get a real sense of connection to the recent past. We have a collection of space toys, for example. In the 1950s and 1960s people were fantastically excited about space travel, so the toys reflect that. We don't take it at all seriously we just love these things.

'David works in television and is particularly interested in anything in the shape of a television. Besides an array of toy televisions, his collection also includes a television-shaped cigarette lighter, cigarette cases, a clock, salt and pepper pots, musical boxes, money boxes, viewers that show pictures on a tiny "television" screen, postcards and posters advertising television programmes, and "spin-off" board games.'

The televisions and related toys and ephemera are really Jane and David's top priority out of all their magpie collections. One reason for this is that the advent of television had such an enormous impact upon society. 'We feel that it's worth trying to build up a record of how popular culture was affected.'

Perhaps the other reason why they have bought so many television-related collectables is that these items are a challenge to find. Therefore, if they do come across something, they can't resist buying it. 'We're definitely guilty of paying over the odds sometimes.'

COLLECTOR'S TIP

'The most collectable Barbies are the brunettes as these were made in smaller numbers than the blondes.'

CHILDREN'S TOYS

With every pair of rose-tinted retrospective spectacles comes a collecting opportunity, which currently means that some old toys are now worth surprisingly large amounts of money. Others, though, are still modestly priced and, second time round, are giving great pleasure to those who collect them.

Judging by the small number of things that were specially made for them, anyone would think that children didn't exist in Britain before and during the eighteenth century. You're also unlikely, unless you're very lucky, to find playthings for children from the early Victorian times. The few toys that have survived from that time were usually beautifully made and worth a small fortune now. They were mostly imported from Germany, which was the centre of the toy industry during the nineteenth century. In Nuremberg alone there were over 400 toymakers in the late nineteenth century.

By the end of the nineteenth century Britain could boast a few great names of her own, such as Britain's and Hornby. The Industrial Revolution enabled much of the change, but there was also a change of attitude. Parents and educationalists alike began to realise that children learn through their play. So, with a keenness to instil moral virtue, board games and toys were produced that often had a Christian message.

By the beginning of the nineteenth century, children's playthings were becoming more commonplace. Smart dolls' house furniture and early mechanical toys were still expensive, but there were also things such as tin soldiers, marbles, spinning tops and hoops to please the poorer families.

Strange as it may seem, toys generally became more affordable from around 1930 as a result of the Wall Street crash. German toymakers lost their most lucrative luxury market, the United States, and had to look elsewhere for business. From then on, the tin toys and the dolls' houses and furniture, for which they were best known, became cheaper and more readily available elsewhere in Europe.

Toys that feature characters from a successful television programme, such as this 1950s Sooty Xylophone, are now looked upon with nostalgia and have become highly collectable.

69

COLLECTING CHILDREN'S TOYS

These days, most of the finest toys from the nineteenth century are in established collections, though you'll still find some in specialist shops. There are many reproductions, such as the porcelain dolls you'll find dressed in pseudo-Victorian clothes, because they have decorative appeal. But these aren't of serious interest to a collector of old toys and won't command the same price.

As toys made before World War II have become rarer and more expensive, collectors are turning to post-war playthings. Hong Kong plastic, wind-up mechanicals, teddies, tin, stuffed toys, Action Man and Barbie – the list goes on. Toy fairs are usually the best places to look. Toys don't often survive unscathed, so quality and condition are important and should be reflected in the price. Barbies or recently made film merchandise won't be worth much if they are 'playworn', but if it's nostalgia you're after, these can be the best bargains.

Certain subjects will be more popular than others because they cross over into other areas. For example, a globe made for a child's dolls' house may be of interest to a map collector. An old Mickey Mouse tin money box will be of interest to a Disney collector, a toy collector and maybe a tin collector. Similarly, a 1960s board game featuring, say, *Thunderbirds* characters from the television series, will appeal to both games enthusiasts and to a *Thunderbirds* collector and perhaps also to a 1960s design buff. This will add a premium to the price.

Nowadays, toys often come in sealed packaging, which makes it difficult to return them to their original boxes once they have been ripped open. So be prepared to display and not play, if investment is your game. Even then, there's no guarantee that any toy will increase in value over time, particularly these days, when it's technically possible to reproduce exactly the same model at a future time, should the need arise.

Toy soldiers are usually made from tin, lead or plastic. This selection belongs to Michael Ellis, a collector who now makes and sells toy soldiers.

MARBLES
Sam McCarthy-Fox

'They're infinite, round, with a mind of their own. They're very tactile and therapeutic and, if you put a whole lot together, it's like having your own stained glass window.' If you thought marbles was just an old-fashioned kids' toy, Sam McCarthy-Fox of Worthing, Sussex can enlighten you.

'The first time I remember playing marbles was in the 1950s when I was a schoolboy in London. The standard marble then was opaque and in different colours. The prize possession was the newly invented Japanese cat's eye – which was clear with a coloured leaf-shape inside.

'There's great variation in old marbles. Each one was hand-made out of molten glass, stretched and twisted like a stick of rock to mix the colours.

'I collect marbles and anything to do with them. I have a kaleidoscope, for example, with a marble in, and "codds" bottles from the 1880s, which have a rubber ring and a marble to make the seal. I also collect newspaper cuttings to do with marbles – Schulz, who draws *Peanuts*, ran a series of cartoons where a kid was playing marbles.

'After a while you get to know what the different colours mean. Some marbles are a softer yellow than the others, which means they came from a particular factory. I collect mostly Victorian glass marbles, which often aren't properly round, but I think they're wonderful. Marbles are fun. I like the recognition when I show them to people; it's as though people have been looking for that lost marble for years!'

DOLLS AND FIGURES

It isn't only the age of a doll that determines how collectable and expensive it is likely to be. The design and method of manufacture, which should be typical of its time, are also important. Generally speaking, reproductions in the clothes of earlier eras will not be as attractive as those dolls that are dressed in the fashions of the day and that are made from materials that were typical.

In Victorian times that would have been a bisque (unglazed pottery) doll appropriately dressed in, say, lace or silk (which may cost from £150 upwards); then in the 1930s you find dolls with pressed felt faces and trouser suits; later, from 1959, Barbie dolls were an innovation. These early Barbie dolls, which had beautifully made clothes, are already widely appreciated. Barbie, Sindy, Action Man and other dolls with an adult shape were brought out around the same time. The early models, now rare in good condition, can be surprisingly expensive. Sindy, the British equivalent of Barbie, is generally still comparatively modestly priced. As in other areas of collecting, the cost of anything that appeals to buyers in the USA tends to be higher. Sasha dolls of the 1970s are also of interest and can fetch a hundred pounds or more, particularly the black Sasha, probably because black dolls were quite rare at that time.

Dolls of all ages, even recently made ones, are

This doll was made to commemorate the Christening of Prince William in 1982. Though decorative and nicely made, it isn't of interest to most serious doll collectors.

collectable – quality and innovative design, together with the general appeal of its appearance is what a collector will look for. So recently made dolls, the first with microchips or those using the latest technology to make them walk, talk and cry, are particularly interesting. The new dolls to look out for would be dressed in up-to-the-minute fashions. These are the ones that will probably hold their appeal in the future.

The first stuffed toys appeared early in the century and these are the ones that now come up at main auction houses. Teddy bears have become enormously popular. They got their name from the US president Teddy Roosevelt, after he refused to shoot a bear while hunting in Mississippi in 1902. Legend has it that a toyshop in New York displayed a stuffed bear labelled 'Teddy's Bear' and from then on the two Teddies were forever linked.

The most famous and costly bears are those made by the German company Steiff. Teddies have become so popular that much has been written about them. Because the early ones can be very valuable and are relatively easy to copy, collectors have to be aware of fakes. Very famous bears and other cuddly toys, particularly those linked to films or television, are also popular with collectors. Early examples of Mickey Mouse (from the 1930s), Rupert, Paddington Bear and the Wombles all evoke nostalgia, which adds to their value.

Felt, velvet and cloth were popular toy-making materials during the 1920s and 1930s, but they're prone to moth damage – the ones that have survived intact and were made by a well known company can sell for hundreds. Those made by Lenci, for example, often fetch hundreds at auction.

Amongst the earliest cheap toys were tin or metal alloy soldiers. Tin ones from the last century are virtually impossible to find and metal alloy, hollow cast ones are thin on the ground too. Collectors have to beware of reproductions in solid metal. Generally these are heavier and obviously newer looking. Yet if you know what to look for there are still valuable old ones waiting to be discovered. Because metal soldiers have become so precious and elusive, collectors in this field have turned to the plastic figures made in the 1940s and later. These can still cost just a pound or two, though for rare ones the price will creep up into double figures. What collectors have to watch out for, with any small old figures, is metal or plastic fatigue. These small figures were mass produced from junk materials and some are in poor condition now, so should cost little.

CARING FOR DOLLS
- Be careful when handling antique dolls as many of them are very fragile. 'Playworn' dolls will lose much of their value.
- Keep new dolls in their original packaging.
- Ask an expert to re-string a doll rather than attempting it yourself. This also applies to re-stuffing cloth dolls.
- Do not repaint a doll's face as this will make it much less attractive to collectors.
- Keep a doll's original costume. If this has been lost, try making a new one from contemporary fabrics.

BOARD GAMES AND PUZZLES

Condition, completeness and subject – these are the three vital ingredients that make a board game or puzzle collectable. The joy of collecting old games is that the demand for them isn't huge and, because there are plenty around, many of them are reasonably priced. The ones that command the highest prices will have that familiar 'cross-over' appeal, which will make them desirable to collectors in more than one field.

Older isn't necessarily more expensive. The quality of the production and the condition of a game or puzzle is more likely to determine its value. A Great Western Railway puzzle was recently sold for around £1,000. It wasn't a particularly early example, and the pieces were made out of cardboard, but it was rare and railways are always a popular subject.

For some collectors, nothing compares to the aesthetic beauty of Victorian games. Some of these were beautifully designed, using early colour printing techniques. But you might occasionally come across a homemade game, which has its own charm and spontaneity, but probably not the same monetary value. The finest and rarest Victorian games will cost you hundreds of pounds, but there are still bargains around, particularly if you're prepared to put up with a little damage or an odd piece missing.

Games that have a long history, such as Fox and Goose (which can be traced back to the Viking invasion) or chess (which has its roots in ancient civilisations) are a massive collecting area. It isn't practical to talk about the values of these games, which vary from a couple of pounds to thousands. As a rough guide, look at whether a classic game is designed in the style of a particular era, and if the pieces are attractive and have artistic credibility.

Common games like Monopoly need to be complete and in good condition to be worth more than a nominal amount.

JIGSAWS
David Cooper

'You have to have a feel for what you collect – I have it for puzzles,' says David Cooper, whose hobby is jigsaws – doing, collecting and restoring them, and making new wooden ones.

'They're a good form of relaxation. I had no idea what a popular hobby jigsaws were at the beginning of this century. There were many manufacturers varying in quality, style and subject. I only realised this when I joined the jigsaw club.

'Many collectors prefer the wooden ones that were made before World War II. After that, cardboard superseded wood.

'I collect mainly wooden puzzles, but also early cardboard, including Mammoth and Good Companion. Prices start at about £5 for a good complete example. That's not expensive for what they are. They're rare, but not worth a lot of money. It's supply and demand – there's very little supply and virtually no demand. Sometimes, though, I've paid over the odds for a puzzle because I've wanted it. And so have most collectors. I am able to restore puzzles with missing pieces and feel I have saved many unique items from being lost forever.'

The invention of the jigsaw puzzle has been attributed to John Spilsbury, a London map-maker, in 1760. The early puzzles, known as dissections, were primarily a teaching aid for children. For decades they were a luxury item and could cost a working man more than a week's wages to buy. Later, after the 1860s, improvements in printing and manufacture techniques reduced the prices, but they were still only affordable to the more affluent. Mostly these dissected pictures depicted geographical, zoological, historical and Biblical subjects.

Today a few rare examples can cost collectors a four figure sum. One such example is Lost in Transit, which was made in the 1930s and given away to GWR employees at their Swindon works.

Jigsaw puzzle collecting is much more popular in the United States, where collectors will pay a lot more for something special. In Britain, you can still buy interesting puzzles at reasonably modest prices. Most collectors prefer puzzles to be complete and in their original boxes.

COLLECTOR'S TIP

'During economic depressions it is the top quality items that keep their value.'

Playing Cards

Major Donald Welsh

'I'VE LEARNED MORE ABOUT HISTORY through collecting playing cards than I did at school,' says Major Donald Welsh who has over 6,000 packs and set up the English Playing Card Society with a fellow enthusiast.

'I'm a magpie. Purely by chance I got into collecting playing cards about twenty-five years ago. I was fed up to the teeth with plastic suitcases and was looking for a leather one. I went into one of those shops that clear houses, and saw three suitcases for £15. One contained 269 packs of playing cards. At first I was collecting cards from all over the world, but I have narrowed it down to English only.

'Ninety-nine per cent of my life is playing cards these days. I'm writing an article about the playing cards of Somerset at the moment. I also recently designed and produced a pack for the Society's fifteenth anniversary. Very few manufacturers produce cards these days, but I found a firm which will do this and also produce a millennium pack. Cards have been out of fashion because of computers and televisions, but now people are realising they can get enjoyment from playing together.

'I'm retired. When I left the services, I thought "let's do something" – not a profession, but not twiddling one's thumbs. So many people who've been in the services, come out and before you can say "Jack Robinson" you're burying them.

'My earliest pack dates from 1688, and has Counts, Viscounts, Dukes, Archbishops and so on. Even now, I'm always finding new cards. I picked up a lovely box of three double-packs, hardly touched, designed by artist William Barribal. I'd wanted them for some time. In the 1930s he produced about eighty different designs. Another recent find was a game of Imperial, a card game for two players, in its original box with rules, produced by Thomas de la Rue in 1881. You also get one-offs, often designed and painted by ladies as a pastime.

'I'm an extrovert and a bore about my cards! I'm always telling people "you want to come and look at my collection, don't you?" Money doesn't come into it with me. The searching and finding is my great joy. In fact, it's often an anti-climax when I've got what I want!'

This copper engraved Nursery Rhyme transformation pack was designed by Donald Welsh for the Society's tenth anniversary in 1993.

Donald Welsh is seen here holding a proof sheet of the Society's fifteenth anniversary pack, designed in 1998. His tie and the picture on the wall behind him also reveal his collecting interest.

COLLECTING PLAYING CARDS

The most popular early designs have been reproduced and can be bought for just a few pounds. Twentieth-century sets are machine made. These days they're plastic coated for durability and ease of cleaning. Cards from the 1930s aren't considered old. Generally speaking you can expect to pay between £25 and £50 for a pre-World War II set with a special face design. An ordinary pack will cost less. Many people will have seen cards issued by cigarette companies from the 1930s. There are so many that a gilt edged double-pack, in the original wrapper, sells for around £12–£15. You might have to pay £60–£100 for a special pre-World War I pack. Old cards that commemorate a particular event will cost even more.

SPORT

Rarely has sport been taken more seriously than it is today. Every main sport – from football to motor racing – has become a multinational industry, and related merchandise is produced specifically for the collecting market. How valuable such items will be in the future remains to be seen. Prices probably won't rise for a long time, because people tend to hold onto things these days.

The charm of sporting memorabilia is that it harks back to a time when games were less self-conscious. The items that have become desirable weren't made with collectors in mind, though much sporting memorabilia is naturally decorative. Trophies made of quality materials or specially made equipment that belonged to a well known sports personality will look good on any mantlepiece. Books, magazines and epehmera all make attractive additions to a collection, particularly if they've been autographed. There are also some pottery figures of famous sportspeople on the market. The ones made before World War II are the most expensive, but modern copies of these are common and are of very little value. Collectors therefore need to be able to tell the difference between the old and the new.

As far as collectables are concerned, the most popular national sport used to be cricket. Recently, however, golf has taken first place. The game's popularity in the USA may have made it the focus of collectors' attention and pushed up prices.

A few sports have long enough histories for mature collectors' markets to exist. In the nineteenth century prints, including cartoons, of cricketers were produced to exploit the interest in the

This scrapbook belonged to tennis champion Mary Healey, who was at the centre of attention in the 1930s. She gave it to her son, Jonathan Cartwright, who has a collection of memorabilia of his mother's tennis career.

sport. These are now judged on both the quality of the print and the importance of the celebrity or team featured. The prints were produced commercially and so many of them are relatively easy to find. Some rarer ones, however, are highly valued and cost hundreds of pounds.

Each sport has its own stellar items. The old leather-covered golf balls, filled with feathers, are so rare now that they can cost over £1,000. You can also expect to pay premium prices for the gloves or championship belts once worn by famous boxers. Many items of decorative art feature sports personalities and these are sometimes expensive because they 'cross over' with other collecting interests. For example, a rare plate or mug that has been painted with a picture of a cricketer would be interesting to both the ceramics collector and a cricketing fan. Competition between the two camps might raise the price at auction.

Though certain celebrities' belongings can fetch enormous sums – such as the bat used by Don Bradman in 1937 when he scored 212 runs for Australia against England – most collectors of sporting memorabilia have more modest tastes. Members of the Cricket Memorabilia Society meet regularly to swap or auction their cigarette cards, photographs and programmes. Autographs of the best cricketers are always sought after and sometimes fetch large sums, but the main point of the society, says president Tony Sheldon, is to foster camaraderie and interest in the game, particularly in the younger members.

Football has become almost as popular as cricket with collectors. The enamelled badges issued by teams to both supporters and players are attractively coloured and designed. There are enough around to make it fun to search them out and they're usually modestly priced once found. A particularly rare one might cost £50, but most can be bought for a pound or two. The Association of Football Badge Collectors is now becoming international. Its secretary, Keith Wilkinson, has been collecting for twenty years, but some overseas members, particularly in Czechoslovakia, have valued them for far longer. Apparently, British supporters used to send them badges during the 1950s.

Any sport that has a long history will have memorabilia to collect. Most of it will be of historical interest rather than of great value, but the kind of things that will always carry a premium are the signed copies of items, personal possessions or equipment of the stars who have entertained throughout the century.

COLLECTOR'S TIP

It's much better to swap a badge for something you haven't got, than to sell it.

KEITH WILKINSON

Bowling Memorabilia
Mary Price

'I HAD ONE BROTHER who was into stamps; another into coins. I finished up with their leftovers. Nowadays I collect things to do with my sport: flat green bowls!' Mary Price of Slough explains how a sporting collection involves soft toys, such as 'Droopy' the lion and 'Dolores' Duck.

'I've been bowling for nearly thirty years. It started when I married my husband Peter and realised I'd be a bowling widow if I didn't take the sport up.

Mary Price, a flat green bowls champion, is pictured on the green beneath the scoreboard. She collects anything to do with her sport.

'Peter and I now run a bowling shop; we play bowls most days, and I won my first trophy at club level in 1970.

'Since then I've travelled the world competing and I've been a member of the England team in three Commonwealth Games. Flat green bowls has only been a

Commonwealth Games sport since 1982; we'll be playing again for England in September.

'You could say that bowling is our lives! The collection is something that has arisen out of the sport. The items are not really about the history of the sport; they're a personal history. When you go to play another team – thirty-three countries play now – there's a ritual of exchanging badges and other memorabilia, specially printed, engraved or embroidered to commemorate the occasion. These could be bookmarks, cuddly toys or a bowls duster. Club badges get swapped, too: an opponent might offer up their club badge in the hope of getting yours.

'When you play at the Commonwealth Games, Atlantic Rim Games or World Bowls, there's usually a special badge struck – so it doesn't take long to amass a collection.

'Souvenir programmes and brochures are also collectable. You have to be a hoarder like me to go the whole way. I also keep menu cards from each trip – and I've got thousands of items, still mostly in boxes. One day I'll get round to displaying them in their full glory, when I persuade my husband to make me a few display cases. He has a much smaller collection of items, particularly from the World Championships in 1992, where he was the umpire.

'Friends collect badges, too, as they go around, so we do swaps. But money doesn't come into it at all.

'They hold special memories for me. For example, last year we won two gold medals at the Atlantic Rim Games– I started crying when I stood on the rostrum to receive them.

'I also have two historic bowls: one bowled on the first day of bowling at our club and another one, about fifty or sixty years old, found when the club was renovated.'

COLLECTING BOWLING MEMORABILIA

The earliest evidence of a bowling green was at Southampton, recorded in 1299. Bowls was played in a haphazard way until the rules were reviewed in the 1840s by a Glasgow solicitor who was a keen player. The Scottish enthusiasm spread to England and abroad until, in 1903, the English Bowling Association was formed. Drake's Pride, of Liverpool, who make bowls, have an archive going back to the beginning of the century, but a collector will find the early memorabilia pretty scarce.

Bowls has always been a low profile sport. The main collectors' pieces are the lapel badges given at championships, which date back to the 1930s. They only cost a pound or two, except the silver ones, which are more valuable.

The gold medals that Mary and her teammates won at the Atlantic Rim Games in 1997.

PASTIMES AS COLLECTABLES

Many people have collections that have grown from their hobby. Model-making, embroidery, pet care and so on are all represented on *Collectors' Lot*. The Kennel Club showed their collection of Crufts memorabilia. Kate Russell, who instigated the 'Leeds Tapestry 2000', inspired 300 of the city's handicraft enthusiasts to contribute to a collection of needlework, beadwork, smocking and lacemaking to celebrate the history of Leeds from its village days to the modern city. One man has dedicated his leisure time to researching and making models of royal carriages, and another showed the gypsy caravan which he'd lovingly restored.

The theatre has attracted its fair share of collectors too. Everything, from sheet music, through to props, costumes and programmes is there to be collected, but few go so far as amateur dramatics director and actress Joy McQuade. Joy has spent a lifetime collecting beautiful period furniture and other items, which she generously and trustingly lends out to amateur thespians – going to see them in action has become a pastime in itself.

It certainly isn't Joy's style, but many theatrical people derive great pleasure from props that they have accumulated on their travels. Props made for the stage can also look quite spectacular when they are transferred to the home environment. They're larger than life, made only for effect, so the fancy bits might be quite crudely, though artistically, painted on or stuck together with glue, but what a dramatic effect they have. You might be able to buy some props if your local theatre has a clear out – but you will have to join a queue behind members of the company, who love to keep such items as mementoes of their performances.

On the other hand, the nice thing about buying old things to use as theatre props is that they don't have to be in fantastic condition – or complete – to be worth buying so you can get the remnants of beautiful things for next to nothing. These are often the sorts of objects a dealer will be happy to part with. They're not ever going to be worth a fortune, and will need some restoration work and tender loving care, but they have potential.

These accessories, a monogrammed gentleman's silk scarf and lady's kid gloves, would have been de rigeur *for theatre goers up to the 1950s. Now they might be more at home backstage in the wardrobe props box.*

AMATEUR DRAMATICS PROPS
Joy McQuade

'I lent my tiger skin to a group performing *Me and My Girl*. I was horrified when one of the teeth dropped out and went flying across the stage.' Joy McQuade of Surrey not only collects props for amateur dramatics – but watches them in action when she lends them out.

'I have four different sizes of chaise longue, lots of hat stands, thirty-odd dolls' houses, chairs, tables and a samovar. We live in a very ramshackle eighteenth-century house full of nooks and crannies. It has around twenty rooms, most of them overflowing with stuff.

'Our lodger had to agree to let us remove bits of her furniture when necessary. Sometimes I ask my husband to stand up so that I can send his chair out for a show!

'I've been involved in amateur dramatics since I was fourteen years old. I've directed several plays, especially open-air Shakespeare, during the forty years that I've been with the Shepperton Players. Shakespeare is my greatest interest. I've played all the major roles, but I've also played the wicked stepmother in pantomime.

'There are about ten local amateur dramatic groups and word spread that I had furniture and props to lend. I think it all started with a left-handed chaise!

'It's not that I go looking for props – we just have loads of old stuff and I am happy to lend it, even the tiger skin, whose owner was shot by my mother-in-law's cousin, Julius Caesar Bulwinkle.

'I don't do it for money. I ask for a donation to charity. I love being involved in amateur dramatics because I didn't train as an actress. I wanted to act, but I suppose I wasn't quite good enough. Instead I got a degree in maths and became a teacher. This way I get to teach all day and act and be involved with theatre all night.'

Joy suggests that if you want to start collecting theatre props, and don't have your own warehouse, then you should fill your home with furniture and other items from junk or charity shops. So don't put up two little pictures – cover empty space with anything that hangs on a wall.

COLLECTOR'S TIP

'There's nothing wrong with buying an honest reproduction as long as the price is right and you like the piece.'

GARDENING

The products of people's leisure activities can be collectables in themselves, priceless to their owners, and inspiration to the rest of us. That's particularly true for one British pastime – gardening.

People have taken pleasure in the aesthetics and the tranquillity of gardens since Ancient Egyptian times. In this country until the nineteenth century, gardening for pleasure was on a grand scale, with famous landscape artists such as Capability Brown working with teams of gardeners.

Gardening became a favourite leisure pursuit amongst the Victorian professional classes and small patches of land burst into colour in urban areas. Tools were mass produced to cater for this. Ladies occupied themselves with picking flowers and pressing them in ornate scrapbooks. There were delicate pruners designed specifically for these genteel activities. The most expensive tools came in special cases and were custom-made by well known cutlers, who ornamented them with coats-of-arms or monograms. They were often presented in sturdy display boxes.

These 'gentleman's' and 'ladies' tools are collectables nowadays – they cost over a hundred pounds and aren't likely to be bought for gardening so much as for display. You can still buy ordinary small tools – such as shears and trowels – cheaply, however, as they have yet to attract collectors.

Around the turn of the twentieth century, social reformers encouraged the development of housing with small gardens for urban workers. Since then, millions have enjoyed expressing their creativity in their gardens.

Perhaps the most practical – and reasonably priced – gardening collectables are the plants themselves. Keen gardeners, of course, are used to swapping cuttings of favourite varieties. Just recently, there has been a revival in interest in the kinds of plants that used to adorn Victorian, or earlier, gardens, but are now rare. These may need a little more research with the help of specialist books.

Other types of garden collections are more expensive. Vintage garden ornaments, for example, have risen in price tremendously in recent years. In fact, when substantial garden sculptures, which have been made for a particular site by a well known artist, do come up for sale, then they might cost many thousands of pounds to buy and relocate. But at least they're not the sort of thing that can be easily stolen.

In the nineteenth century smaller ornaments were made, which are now appreciated for their detailed workmanship. Items such as

COLLECTOR'S TIP

'People sometimes get carried away at auctions. Two keen collectors can push up the price until one of them pays well over the odds.'

GARDEN GNOMES
Ann Atkins

'I think a quality gnome stands up very well as a sculpture,' says Ann Atkins, who has around seventy in her collection at the Gnome Reserve and Wildflower Garden in North Devon. 'Some are beautifully made, with good detail and colour, and have survived the hazards of winters and children. Old gnomes sometimes come up at auction and, as the demand is not so great, you may be able to buy them fairly cheaply, but I'd certainly expect to pay well over £100 for a full sized, good quality Victorian gnome, sometimes several hundred. Once housed, people tend to treat them as one of the family, so gnomes don't often come up for sale.'

Gnomes are thought to have been introduced to Britain by the Victorian eccentric Sir Charles Isham, who was a keen gardener. He built a huge rockery with moats, crystal caves, canyons and dwarf variety shrubs and trees at his home, Lamport Hall, in Northamptonshire. Sir Charles thought it would be fun to have colourful gnomes to inhabit the rockery, so he sent off to the Heissner pottery in Nuremberg for some. The terracotta gnomes started a craze and by the end of the nineteenth century over a million were being imported into Britain each year. No-one is sure what happened to Sir Charles's gnomes after his death, but they were all thought to have been lost. Then during repair work after World War II an original gnome was found hidden in a cave. It now lives in solitary splendour under a glass dome in the library of Lamport Hall.

Most of the Victorian gnomes you'll see were made in Germany or Czechoslovakia. They're hollow terracotta and can be as tall as 30 in (80 cm). New gnomes are generally far cheaper – prices start at £2.50. German terracotta ones are still produced in traditional styles. They sometimes come up at fairs, but should be very much cheaper than the originals.

This gnome, and the one overleaf, is Victorian, German, handpainted and made of terracotta.

mid-height statues, terracotta planters, sundials and stone sculptures now fetch very good prices. If you've paid something in the region of three thousand pounds or more for one (as you might from a specialist dealer), you should think twice about putting it out in your garden – many have been stolen in recent years.

Garden ornaments were produced in lead, cast-iron, terracotta and stone. They were in huge demand during the nineteenth century, and companies opened all over Britain to produce them.

Today, there are many much cheaper reproductions around, though these can still cost hundreds of pounds at garden centres. The reproductions will be obvious to a trained eye because they won't have the same patina. Lead, for instance, takes on a whitish appearance with weathering, which is attractive to a collector.

Garden gnomes are popular collectables today, especially the old ones. The first mention of garden gnomes was by the German scientist Paracelsus in his book *De Nymphis*, which was published in 1648. From 1871 they were imported here from German potteries, notably Heissner, who supplied half of the enormous British market. Nowadays, colourful old gnomes are valuable enough to need to be taken care of indoors, so they're the ideal conservatory pet.

With the new, reasonably priced oddities and ornaments available from garden centres, a little creative thinking can produce a magical place. Designer Malcolm Tempest of North Yorkshire created a garden which people visit to enjoy the novelty and tranquillity. He drew inspiration from the past to create a collection of modern day artefacts, including a glass pyramid, a maze and an underground grotto with sculptures. Malcolm's collection isn't of the past. It is about creativity, fantasy and imagination – three important ingredients when building any good collection.

Gnomes are often given suitable jobs to do in the garden – possibly a form of wishful thinking on the owner's part. This little chap is carrying some flowerpots, in order to do some potting out.

GARDENING TOOLS
David Bridgewater

'Over the past five or six years I've accumulated enough of the paraphernalia of gardening to make a great museum,' says David Bridgewater, collector and antiques dealer, whose most recent enthusiasm is for gardening tools. 'I collect to sell, but I've always had the collecting bug. Everything I collect is useful. If I need a spade, I'll grab one off the wall.

'One of the secrets of collecting, if you're a short-term collector like me, is to buy before it becomes fashionable and the prices creep up. I don't buy lawnmowers because there are already lots of people interested in them. You have to anticipate what's happening, keep in touch with the *zeitgeist*, which gets more difficult as you get older.

'I'm a sucker for garden centres and bookshops. I'm looking to maximise on what I sell, which includes garden pots. It's not done for pure collecting reasons. You put in a small plant, which costs very little, and within a year it's filled the pot, which makes it come alive. In fact, plants are the ideal collectable if you're looking for a good investment.

'I don't think I'll tire of collecting – you can't teach an old dog new tricks. But I like to think that once I've bought something and found out about it, it's inside of me and I've cured myself of it – then I part with it.'

You might be able to buy a cheap new spade at the local hardware store, but it won't have a history. In 1880, for example, Brades, of Sheffield made eighty different patterns of spade in five different sizes. Each different region had its own particular shape, depending on the type of soil or the people who were working with it. You might pay £35–£60 for such a spade these days from a dealer.

In the seventeenth century specialised gardening tools were custom made by blacksmiths to fit each gardener's hand. Iron was expensive, so broken tools were melted down and recycled, which is why they're rare today. Gardeners took great care of their tools and often decorated them with flowers, scrolls or religious mottos. Professionals would travel from place to place with their own tool kits.

COLLECTOR'S TIP

'Learn to recognise the feel of quality by handling pieces in good collections or shops.'

CHAPTER FIVE

The Way We Were

Memorabilia

Any objects that provoke a memory of how people used to live, or which marks a special event, can be called memorabilia. Souvenirs of all sorts – letters, pictures, toys, china and personal possessions – become precious clues in a quest to build pictures of a lost time.

The study of memorabilia is the study of people – often famous or important people, but equally it can concern the habits of ordinary folk. There are thousands of collectors who make it their business to be the custodians of our collective memory. Their collections remind us that although many of us see the past as an endless cycle of golden summers and cosy winter evenings by the fire, the reality was often much more harsh.

Collectors are interested in the flotsam and jetsam of people's lives and often they become extremely knowledgeable about their chosen subject. They explore the history of every item that they come across and enjoy the unique story that each one tells. It's as though collectors use a mixture of nostalgia and curiosity to create time capsules that are respectful of the day-to-day stuff of life. Sharing those 'capsules' helps to shed a light on the past and put it into perspective. It can also be a great source of fun. For the collectors themselves, the items that they painstakingly gather together can become a way of connecting with people in the present as well as the past.

> ### COLLECTOR'S TIP
>
> *'If you show a friendly curiosity people are very generous with their memories. You learn a lot that way.'*
>
> CHRISTOPHER BUTLER

It isn't unusual for someone to begin a collection based on family history or a deep nostalgia for childhood. Most of us have at least the beginnings of such a collection tucked away in the back of a cupboard. Births, deaths and marriages in the family, holidays that we have enjoyed and wars that we have lived through are represented through the ephemeral items of each successive generation. Invitation cards and postcards, bus tickets and bibles, wedding veils and war medals can all invoke strong personal and universal memories. Diverse objects sit easily with one another in these eclectic collections. Things needn't cost a lot, though sometimes they do. The pleasure and purpose lies in seeking out and exploring a theme.

Half the fun is in arranging and sorting a collection. The rest is in foraging at markets or collectors' fairs, getting to know others who have the same interest, maybe contacting a specialist club, and finding information in museums and libraries.

One theme that runs through many of the collectors in this chapter is that they are preserving the recent, living past. Whether they collect memorabilia from World War II, souvenirs of the royal family or funeral ephemera, their collections still have the ability to move the general public.

Everyday items form the backbone of Christopher Butler's collection of World War II memorabilia (see pages 98–9).

FINDING MEMORABILIA

Even though some of these collectables can be quite valuable, memorabilia doesn't warrant a department to itself at any of the main auction houses. Such a gamut of items might be described as memorabilia that it's difficult to put them into any one category.

Large and important collections do come up from time to time, and they are often sold in specially organised sales by the most appropriate department in the auction house. For example, when a substantial amount of political memorabilia came up at Phillips, one of the large auction houses, it was the responsibility of the ceramics department because many items were pots of one sort or another. In another instance, it may become the book department's responsibility, especially if autographs and printed material feature heavily. Otherwise, a collector might find a commemorative brooch in a jewellery sale, an interesting signed photograph in a book sale, an item of clothing in the textile department and so on.

No one can dictate or set standards for these collectables. They turn up in all sorts of places; the quality of the item itself is usually regarded as secondary to its value as a piece of history. You'll soon find out which items are easily found and which are rarer. Most of those people we spoke to said that once they had let people know about their special interest they often had things passed on to them by friends, family or local dealers. Sadly, others said that they had occasionally come across a seller who, knowing of their special interest, had hiked up the price.

Prices swing with the economy, too. One thing that tends to happen is that when the general economy takes a turn for the worse, people try to sell on their collections. It becomes a 'buyers' market' and prices fall.

Clearly, some things are going to be quite expensive. Spurred on by the mushrooming of television and radio programmes, books and magazines about collecting, prices have crept up in just about every field. Price is obviously demand-led, so the more people who are chasing a scarce object the higher the price will be. The skill is in judging what is really in demand and deciding if a thing is worth the price to you personally. Everyone has a budget, and most of us find it helpful to draw a line before getting carried away at an auction or fair.

One collector who has mastered this is Christopher Butler, who collects World War II memorabilia (*see pages 98–9*). 'I limit myself at car boots and jumbles to spending £10, but if there's something I really want, I'll pay extra. I haven't been to any big auctions. I go to

COLLECTOR'S TIP

'A collector should not forget that today's items will, one day, be of importance.'

JULIAN LITTEN

the aerojumbles, which are advertised in military magazines such as *Flypast*. They happen a couple of times a year.'

Christopher also acknowledges the importance of knowing your subject inside out if you are to be successful over a long time. 'I think I'm a typical collector. I enjoy finding a bargain and then holding a piece of history in my hand. I think car boot sales are brilliant, especially now I know what I'm looking for, through reading books and making mistakes over time.'

Some things are quite rare, but won't be expensive because so few people want them. The usual advice may not be cut and dried, but it's a good measure to use. Buy what you're attracted to, for a price that you can afford. These types of collections don't hold their value in the same way as top quality decorative arts might. So the general rule is, don't buy for investment, particularly in this field, because no one can reliably predict whether prices will rise or fall. (You'll find more about the miscellany of things that might fall under the heading of memorabilia elsewhere in the book.)

World War II badges, which form part of Christopher Butler's collection.

This fork was made to commemorate the coronation of Edward VIII in 1937. Edward abdicated, but the coronation date remained the same for his brother, George VI.

COMMEMORATIVES

'An item made for the public at large to mark an event contemporary with the times in which it was made.' This was a Victorian historian's definition of a commemorative and one which Steven Jackson, Secretary of the Commemorative Collectors' Society, often quotes when he addresses groups of keen collectors. 'Think of any human activity and it's odds on that there's a commemorative to record it – politics, sport, theatre, royalty – anything that has a following,' says Steven's wife Nancy. The couple are currently building up a research archive of commemoratives. 'Beauty is in the eye of the beholder, and what turns one person on might be horrible to someone else. Pretty well anything goes. At their best, commemoratives are great fun. They're a visual form of history, recorded for posterity, sometimes in a very amusing way.'

Most commemoratives are pottery, but you'll also find glassware, silver, plastic, badges, bookmarks, textiles, printed material, programmes, special edition magazines – such as the *Illustrated London News* – and so on. These days media products, tapes and videos, have entered the market, whereas some items, handkerchiefs for example, are becoming obsolete.

Recent commemoratives might feature events as diverse as the Spice Girls' tour of India, the general election, the Festival of Britain or the opening of a musical in the West End. Most, however, still feature royalty, a state visit for example.

Souvenirs are not usually commemoratives although they can unintentionally record an important event. One such example is the nursery pictures taken by photographer Marcus Adams of young Princess Elizabeth, which were transferred onto sets of pottery. As Nancy explains, 'At the time no-one expected her to become queen. Anniversaries are also a grey area. There are companies that specialise in producing items to mark one hundred years since a birth, for example, or twenty-five years since an event. Though some are genuine commemoratives, many of these are too obscure to be taken seriously and they would be low on the list for collectors. They are really more of a marketing exercise by the company than a genuine commemorative.'

The limited edition market, which came into its own in the mid-1960s, has its place, but the general advice is to buy because you want to live with an item, not for investment purposes. They may be difficult to sell on and are not likely to increase greatly in value.

Commemoratives have come a long way since 1660, when the small Delft mug was made for the coronation of Charles II.

Interestingly, the king's picture was originally intended to be Oliver Cromwell but with the return of the monarchy the artist hastily altered it to resemble Charles. It isn't unusual for items of this age, made before mass production, to sell for £10,000 or more at auction. Happily not all commemorative pottery is so far out of reach. From the 1850s it was mass produced. The longevity and popularity of Queen Victoria ensured that millions of transfer-printed plates and jugs commemorated both her Golden and Diamond Jubilees. They were given away at parties for the children of the poor. They're now worth around £10. Press-moulded glass plates of the same age cost about £10–£20. A range of products were made for Prince Albert's 'big idea', The Great Exhibition of 1851, which was envisaged as the launchpad for British Industry. And manufacturers in all fields, then as now, were not slow to trade on patriotic pride.

Many different companies have since produced items to record national events – from horseraces to cross channel flights. It's a huge subject with great variations in prices. By and large any twentieth-century commemoratives are worth little. An item usually has to be of exceptional quality, or date back to the last century to command a better price. So you'd still find 1937 abdication mugs for £10, unless it was the very one owned by the Windsors themselves, which was sold for over a thousand dollars recently.

This plate was issued after the divorce of Diana, Princess of Wales in 1996.

COLLECTOR'S TIP

'Pieces that feature portraits are more likely to rise in the collectability stakes than those bearing royal arms.'

STEVEN JACKSON

Margaret had just got planning permission to build an extra room for the Queen Mother, when she heard that Diana had died. She has now dedicated the new lounge to the Princess of Wales.

Royal Memorabilia

Margaret Tyler

'I'VE ALWAYS LOVED THE THEATRE and you can't get much more dramatic than the Royal Family,' says Margaret Tyler of Middlesex, who has been dubbed Britain's 'loyal-est' Royalist.

'My interest in the royal family began when I was a child. I grew up an only child in the Forest of Dean. I think I saw them as the ideal family, and there were an awful lot of them.

'I started collecting in 1976, when I had my own children and was helping out at a school jumble sale. I borrowed two-and-a-half pence to buy a small glass dish with the Queen's head in the centre. From there on it just took off until now I have over 5,000 items, including sixteen concrete corgis and a garden gnome of Prince Charles. Some date back to the reign of Queen Victoria. I haunt car boot sales and charity shops.

'I have four children, two grandchildren and a full-time job at the Down's Syndrome

Visitors to Margaret's house can have breakfast with the Queen and Prince Philip. Cardboard cut-outs of members of the royal family are complemented by a dresser filled with plates and mugs commemorating royal weddings and jubilees.

Association. But I just love my collection. I collect much more since I've been divorced. I've certainly made lots of friends from my interest. Now I do Royal Bed and Breakfast and get visitors from as far away as Japan. When Edward VIII would have been one hundred years old, I held a party at home and played a recording of his abdication speech.

'I honestly think that I'll be doing it until the day that I die.'

COLLECTING ROYAL MEMORABILIA

It's easy and relatively cheap to start a collection of royal souvenirs made this century, but you might have to wait aeons before they appreciate in value – charity shops and car boot sales are full of recently made memorabilia. Special edition newspapers or 1953 coronation programmes can be found for around £2, but the more rare *Illustrated London News* special edition, 'Diamond Jubilee 1897' might cost around £20.

Jubilee souvenirs were often regarded as family heirlooms, but a lot of them were produced and their value today is still modest. On the other hand, items owned by a member of the royal family, which occasionally come up for sale, are likely to be costly.

Unusual, recently made souvenirs are the mugs satirising Prince Charles and published by *Private Eye*: 'Royal Divorce' or the 'Annus Horribilis'. If any royal collectables are to go up in value, these are the ones to watch.

This money box is shaped like a Corgi, the Queen's favourite breed of dog.

MEDALS AND COMMEMORATIVE COINS

Medals and decorations are collectable for their social history. The stories of great bravery that often accompany one of the highest awards attract a great deal of interest amongst collectors. This is why a Victoria Cross belonging to a particularly well known person will sell for thousands, while a World War II service medal will cost only a few pounds due to the number awarded and the fact that people weren't individually named. Yet they are rich in history and memories for the soldiers and their families who own them. The first time that medals were awarded to all the ranks was after the Battle of Waterloo (1815). During World War I each decoration was engraved with the soldier's name. The price that a medal sells for today will reflect who owned it and their regiment. For example, the Scots Grey Regiment medal is worth considerably more than the Royal Artillery one. The highest British decoration for conspicuous bravery in the face of the enemy awarded to British and Commonwealth armed forces is the Victoria Cross (VC). This bronze medal is 1.5 in (4 cm) in diameter and has a crimson ribbon. It was instituted by Queen Victoria in 1856.

The George Cross is an award particularly given to civilians, but also to military personnel, for gallant acts. In June 1997, for example, it was awarded to Lisa Potts for her bravery in defending her Wolverhampton infants' class from the machete blows of Horrett Campbell. The award was instigated by King George VI in 1940, during the blitz of World War II. The medals rarely come up for sale, but if one was given to someone involved in an emotive, historical incident, such as the Dambusters, it could cost £20,000. One given to an airforce officer for gallantry would be expected to net around £4,000 to £5,000 at auction.

Commemorative coins have been produced in large numbers during the last fifty years, but haven't turned out to be very good investments yet. For example, a 1951 Festival of Britain coin is still only worth £1.50 today. The only recently struck coin to have doubled in value is the one issued for the 1981 wedding of Prince Charles and Lady Diana Spencer – and that's only worth 50p! Package coins, too, are normally valued by the weight of their gold or silver. These types of commemoratives are fine as souvenirs of an event, but their wealth is in history rather than cash.

The coin on the left was produced to celebrate Queen Elizabeth II's Silver Jubilee in 1977. That on the right was issued in 1897 on the Diamond Jubilee of Queen Victoria.

PRISONER OF WAR ART
Ray Newell

'A German guard posed for me once while other British Prisoners of War were digging an escape tunnel, just a few feet below us.' Ray Newell of Hertfordshire, spent three years in PoW camps in Germany and Italy during World War II. His graphic record of that time has recently been exhibited.

'I was an artilleryman in North Africa, captured after the fall of Tobruk and imprisoned at first in Benghazi. I'd been an art student so I began sketching on paybooks, in Bibles and on the inside covers of novels – in exchange for food and cigarettes. The malnutrition was such that at one point I only weighed seven-and-a-half stone [47.6 kg]. We would often have what we called "Benghazi blackouts" when we stood up. One of the pictures shows a Russian PoW scavenging for fat in empty tins in the rubbish area.

'Over time, I was moved to Italy and eventually to Germany where art supplies came in bulk Red Cross parcels from Britain. I became the art teacher of Stalag IVB, 56 miles (90 km) south of Berlin. There were thousands of prisoners there from forty different nations. I did portraits of every nationality. One picture in the exhibition is done with a penknife because, although the oil paints arrived, the brushes were mislaid.

'I was freed by the Russians in 1945. We were only allowed to bring back one pack so I threw away my belongings and just brought the drawings, which I kept at home for the next forty years. I retired as a commercial artist in 1986 and got a voluntary job helping curators in the Tower of London armouries, doing things like drawing marks on bayonets. They asked me if I could illustrate some of their articles and books, so I showed them four of my drawings to prove I could do it. They said they'd love to exhibit them at their vast new museum in Leeds and then at Fort Nelson in Portsmouth.

'I was recording these PoWs at a time when nobody was interested in them. Now eighty of the drawings are on show – and people are fascinated. I even had a phone call from someone who was digging that escape tunnel while I was drawing!'

> **COLLECTOR'S TIP**
>
> *'Try to keep good records of where and when you bought something and what you know of its history.'*

World War II Memorabilia

Christopher Butler

'I LOVE WATCHING FILMS SET IN WARTIME. A love scene was so much cosier then,' says Christopher Butler, aged thirty-nine, of Sussex. In honour of the times, he collects everything to do with World War II from sweetheart brooches to tin helmets.

'My father was in the navy during the war. He sailed on the *Cleopatra* into Singapore after it was liberated. When I was nine or ten my gran used to tell me stories about her and my mum being bombed in the war, about drinking cocoa in the Morrison shelter during raids, and coming upstairs to find the ceiling down and doors blown in.

'In the 1960s, dad took me to Tangmere to see a spitfire at the gate. Now I'm a volunteer at the museum there. I collect anything from the 1940s. I recently went to an antiques fair at Goodwood race track. I picked up a suitcase for £5. When I got it home it had sixty items from the 1940s in it: knitting and dress patterns, wartime shampoo (the powder kind that you mix up), recipe books and, right at the bottom, a pair of Christian Dior war-time stockings. The things remind me of a time when people helped each other out.

'I get a great response to my collection, especially from widows and widowers. I've

Christopher is pictured with some of his World War II memorabilia. 'Hamish' Mahaddie's photo is to his right, and that of Christobel Leighton Porter, the model for the Jane cartoons, is top centre.

COLLECTING WORLD WAR II MEMORABILIA

The service personnel, those left behind on the home front, children who were evacuees and conscientious objectors all have wartime stories to tell. Everyone lived their own personal war between 1939 and 1945. Families still have their own archives, be it bundles of letters, telegrams, ration books or clothes.

Wartime memorabilia regularly turns up at collectors' fairs. The items that command high prices are things of intrinsic value. An original RAF flying jacket, the style and provenance of which might appeal to a young person, rarer documents marking particular wartime events, which may come up at auction, letters between well known writers and the belongings of a well known personality are all sought after.

Prices will depend on who is buying and selling and how scarce and interesting an item is. As those who fought in the war pass on their memorabilia to the next generation, so more items become available to collectors. This makes the financial value very difficult to predict.

These sew-on badges were to identify those men and women who stayed at home and guarded other civilians from attack.

started giving talks in schools, wearing an ARP (Air Raid Protection) tin hat.

My favourite part of the collection is the sweetheart brooches. It would be nice to find out the stories behind them.

'The generation that fought for us in the war is quite elderly now, so I want to talk to people before it's too late.

'One man I really admired was Group Captain T.G. "Hamish" Mahaddie. He chose people for the Pathfinder force, alongside "Bomber" Harris. It's sad to think that 55,000 bomber crew didn't come back. Their average age was only twenty-two.'

THE HOLIDAY SPIRIT

Many people find that their most vivid and poignant memories are of the holidays that they experienced, particularly as · children, but also as adults. Although nowadays we take going on holiday for granted, this wasn't always the case. The tourism pioneer Thomas Cook organised his first day trip in 1841. It was a temperance train ride from Leicester to Loughborough and cost a shilling. By 1849 he was organising three-day trips to the seaside at Scarborough and in 1866 arranged the first tour to Niagara Falls.

Wealthy families, including the new generation of successful industrialists and their children, were fortunate enough to be able to embark on a 'Grand Tour' of Europe, Egypt or other exotic destinations around the British Empire. The local populations were quick to realise the potential of making souvenirs. Over time, some of these have become valuable antiques, appreciated for their workmanship and the quality of the materials. One such example is the Japanese-made Noretaki china and other items in Richard Lowe's Egyptiana collection (*see page 13*). Other souvenirs were poorly made and, in spite of their age, still don't command great prices. Jewellery, trinkets, pottery and miscellaneous trifles often come under the hammer at local salerooms and occasionally the main auction houses have what they term 'Grand Tour' sales.

Shell ornaments have been popular holiday souvenirs since Victorian times.

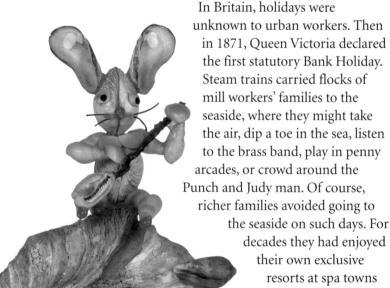

In Britain, holidays were unknown to urban workers. Then in 1871, Queen Victoria declared the first statutory Bank Holiday. Steam trains carried flocks of mill workers' families to the seaside, where they might take the air, dip a toe in the sea, listen to the brass band, play in penny arcades, or crowd around the Punch and Judy man. Of course, richer families avoided going to the seaside on such days. For decades they had enjoyed their own exclusive resorts at spa towns such as Tunbridge Wells and Bath.

GOSS POTTERY
Michael Fish

'William Henry Goss started it all,' explains television weather presenter Michael Fish, 'but then other firms realised that people liked to buy crested china at the seaside, so they jumped on the bandwagon. Dozens of companies started to make it but none of them were of the same quality as Goss.'

Victorian Staffordshire potter and businessman William Henry Goss invented coats of arms for towns that had none and, with his son Adolphus, sold them to holiday resorts on small pieces of souvenir china. Michael Fish has several hundred pieces of china manufactured by Goss for the tourist trade. He specialises not only in 'Eastbourne' Goss but those stamped 'R. Fish', meaning that they were sold at his grandfather's Eastbourne newsagent's. It all started when the Fish family were browsing at an antiques fair, and his daughter turned up a piece of Eastbourne Goss to find her great-grandfather's stamp underneath.

Souvenir pottery in general was made as early as the mid-nineteenth century. If you like this kind of thing, it can be fun to collect, and relatively inexpensive although it depends what you aim for. It's a developed collecting area, so there are price guides which give collectors a good idea of relative values.

In Britain, the souvenir market was less grand than on the continent where a wealth of luxury purchases were available. Cheap and cheerful keepsakes were produced to take home and put on the mantelpiece. They were mainly made out of pottery and often had the name of the town written on them. Views of the coastline were also popular. Most of these souvenirs would have been imported from Germany or made in the Staffordshire town of Stoke-on-Trent. Some were given away as prizes at the fair – fairings, as they're now called, can be quite highly valued today.

Collectors might also come across a range of homemade souvenirs dating from Victorian times. Shells, pebbles, hair and flowers, all natural materials, were gathered to make keepsakes of a trip. The price a collector would expect to pay for such items these days will depend very much on the quality of the work and the appeal of the subject.

COLLECTOR'S TIP

'Forged pieces of Goss are quite rare, but they do exist. A simple test is to scratch the marking on the bottom with your fingernail. If it's a fake it should come off quite easily.'

The holiday camp entrepreneur Billy Butlin started his business in 1937. His Butlins chain offered family holidays where the food, accommodation and entertainment were all included in the price. When the war broke out in 1939 he made a deal with the British government to hand his resorts at Filey, Clacton, Skegness and Pwllheli over to the armed forces. These sites became barracks until after the war.

At a time when people first started getting paid for an annual holiday, breaks at Butlins only cost a week's wages and families came in droves. The daily timetable was quite regimented, with set times for waking up, meals and amusements, but that suited many people who were used to being in the armed forces or living by the factory horn.

Holiday camp souvenirs are ten-a-penny and so are likely to be quite cheap. The ones that have appeal to collectors in other fields, such as the costume that Mark Goddard bought from the *Hi-de-Hi* television programme, or a piece of Goss or other quality pottery, will cost more.

This Butlin Holiday Picture was taken during the 1950s on the beach at Skegness.

HOLIDAY EPHEMERA
Mark Goddard

'Anyone who's got a passion about something is worth listening to,' says Mark Goddard who, after fourteen years working as an Entertainments Manager on holiday camps, tells their unique story through the objects he's saved.

'After my first couple of seasons at Pontins in 1984 and 1985, I realised something very basic – everything had Pontins written on it! I've since worked for Warners and collected important items there, and found Butlins stuff at car boot sales and antique fairs.

'If you've got something you're enthusiastic about, people will relate to it. This matters when you work at a holiday camp. My collection always brings a smile to the face and a happy memory from people, even the ones who went once to a camp and said "never again". It gives me an "in" to conversations; a reason to sit and chat for half an hour.

'I think the objects tell a history, sometimes very clearly. For example, I've got postcards that tell you what the weather was like in a given week of a given year. The people who wrote on those cards are giving a record of what sort of time they were having.

'The corniness and tackiness appeal to me. Holiday camps are not snooty. I've picked things up at car boot sales for 50p or £1. During the recession, people were offloading their collections. I bought £250 worth of badges once, as someone needed the money and I wanted his badges.

'There are things I have bought with an idea to sell, but my gut feeling stops me. I find it difficult to offload anything unless I do a swap for a missing link in the collection. There are some 1955 glass tankards with Butlins written on them, for example, which were given out each Christmas to the guests. I'm looking for one that would give me the complete set. Every Butlins centre used to have a bronze bust of Billy Butlin; if one of those ever came up, I'd love to get hold of it. One of my best items is the Spike Dixon (Jeffrey Holland) uniform from the television series *Hi-De-Hi*. I bought it at a BBC auction.'

COLLECTOR'S TIP

'Collecting is about enthusiasm. Collectors recognise a kindred spirit.'

MARK GODDARD

REJECTAMENTA
Stella Mitchell

'I'm looking at the past through the flotsam and jetsam that's been left behind,' says Stella Mitchell of Chichester, West Sussex. So 'accumulative' is her personality that she's ended up with her own personal museum of 'things that other people threw away'.

'Every spare penny I've had for the last twenty-five years has gone on my collection. My first husband never understood why all my money was going to charity shops and the marriage collapsed under all the clutter. Dressed shop dummies on the stairs are not to everyone's taste.

'Ten years ago I married a man who supported me in leaving my job as a postwoman, and setting up Rejectamenta – the Nostalgia Centre. Now the collection's housed in a huge converted glasshouse at Earnley, near Chichester. It spans twenty-six different sections of twentieth-century life: from cosmetics to travel, healthcare to wartime, kitchen equipment to costume.

'I started with ephemera: paper bags, receipts, Woolworth's "Winfield" labels, vests and strange pieces of underwear. Then I moved on to consumer durables, such as washers, cookers, television sets and record players.

'Back in the 1970s, as an art student, I used "nostalgia" as a theme for my degree work – I'd arrange things in boxes, rather like the displays I do now in the museum. I realised how much I loved the "pop-art" era – for example, Peter Blake's *Toyshop* assembled in 1962. I loved the Hong Kong type toys from the 1950s, the ones I was not allowed to have when I was a child. Barbara Hulanicki of Biba was the major 1960s stylist for me – she looked at her business in such an artistic way, right down to the labels on the clothes. She was an undeniable influence.

'I'm fascinated at how things evolve. I've got a wallpaper trimmer, for example, which you needed in the days when machines couldn't print wallpaper right to the edges. So you had to trim your piece before you hung it. A simple object sums up how in the past "ignorance was bliss."'

COLLECTOR'S TIP

'The only real guide is to ask yourself if the asking price is worth it to you, personally.'

DAVID COOPER

FLOTSAM AND JETSAM

Collections can be founded on any number of themes, and they aren't always rooted far in the past. There are those who see everyday disposables in a different light, recognising the value of what other people discard.

Collector Stella Mitchell, of Chichester, is an inspiration to anyone who finds it difficult to throw out the things they don't use or need. She makes works of art out of what otherwise might have been put in the bin, and has created a series of museum pieces that people will happily pay to look at.

You might even say that Stella has perfected the art of collecting, in that she can see beauty and potential in the ordinariness of the present. Ephemera are, by definition, of their time, and everything that Stella uses in her displays shows its age. A supermarket receipt, a trinket or toy, an entrance ticket or an exercise book could bring memories flooding back. You might see the people who collect these memorabilia as 'rescuers' of a current generation: they see stories in everything and anything.

A typical tableau by Stella Mitchell displays various television ephemera. Games from tie-ins are propped up against ancient sets and TV dinner trays.

Funeral Ephemera
Julian Litten

'DEATH IS GENERIC TO EVERYMAN. What is everybody's is nobody's – life is ephemeral.' So speaks the philosophical Julian Litten of East London. He nevertheless seeks out the tangibles of the ephemeral in the pursuit of the history of the English funeral, from 1650 to 1900.

'Mine is a collection that has reached fruition over thirty years. It started in the 1960s, when I was required to provide a report on a burial vault. When research libraries drew a blank I decided to seek and amass for myself artefacts on the history of the English funeral. Since then I've collected everything from copies of funeral furnishers' catalogues to undertakers' ledgers, coffin furniture and shrouds. It's a unique record,

Julian Litten has spent the last thirty years collecting funeral ephemera. However, he does not live with his collection – all 3,000 objects have been archived and stored away.

resulting in 3,000 objects, ranging from mourning stationery to death masks.

'Money does not come into my collecting – I can't drive a bargain – and I'm more of a clinical academic than a collector as such, although I don't desire to own every known trade journal or death mask, rather examples of each category for the record.

'There is also a scarcity factor. Catalogues devoted to mourning cards, for example, were rarely retained by the trade once superseded, and yet their sentimental poetry

Julian's collection includes miniature coffins for undertakers to show to families at home and display cards of coffin linings.

and verse are particularly quaint.

'I know of five others who collect as widely as I do and we frequently assist one another by locating or exchanging items.

'As President of the Friends of Kensal Green Cemetery in north-west London I am kept reasonably busy finding monies to assist the General Cemetery Company to conserve its listed buildings and monuments and to retrieve the original landscape.

'I now have a vault there which, due to its expense, I acquired over a number of years. I expect that my funeral will be nineteenth century in flavour – although I do not want horses – and that I will be dressed in a shroud from my own collection, and, of course, a triple coffin of wood, lead and wood will be required.'

Broadsheets used to be issued giving details of who attended royal and distinguished funerals.

COLLECTING FUNERAL EPHEMERA

Before around 1625, shroud burial was the norm and coffins were used only for the wealthy, but with the introduction of the funeral trade in the mid-seventeenth century came commercialism. Funerals were tailored according to social status, with the period 1725–75 marking the zenith of the English funeral. By the 1850s, church cemeteries in urban areas were overcrowded. It wasn't unusual to find a grave re-used less than a year after a burial. Joint stock cemetery companies had been established in the 1830s to buy up areas of land for use as extensions to churchyards. Their success led to the municipal cemeteries that are still used today. Cremation was made legal in 1902.

'Green' funerals re-appeared in the 1870s with the advent of basketwork, wicker and papier-mâché coffins sold by the Earth-to-Earth Company. By the 1880s there was a backlash against the pomp of the 'six-in-hand' multi-plumed sable funeral. Elaborate funerals became non-U and were sold down to the working classes. Thus that which the Victorian East Ender thought was 'posh' had been abandoned by the upper classes who preferred a less ostentatious parade.

A Victorian shroud from Julian's collection.

CHAPTER SIX

Time and Technology

Mechanical Objects

Inventors and designers in the twentieth century have worked at a frenzied pace to change the face of the world. Whole new collecting areas have evolved, such as electrical goods, cars, televisions and computers. These collections provide a snapshot of modern advances, and continue a fine tradition of collating mechanical objects.

P eople at the end of the nineteenth century must have looked back on a century of Industrial Revolution with awe. Yet they could never have imagined the remarkable material progress that was to come. The efforts of the twentieth century's 'movers and shakers', including scientists, inventors and designers, have pushed each generation's tolerance of change to its limits, and sometimes beyond. For some collectors, the joy of their collection is in the story it tells of how these inventions evolved.

Technology and design go hand in hand, so much so that it's often difficult to say whether a pocket watch is best described as a piece of jewellery or a mechanism; whether a kettle is pure technology or partly decorative art. But that's not an issue for those who appreciate all aspects of their chosen collectable. For them, technology, design and social history merge. An item doesn't have to be expensive to hold the attention of a collector, but these days the combination of aesthetics and technical excellence doesn't come cheap.

> ### COLLECTOR'S TIP
>
> *'Value depends on "willing buyer, willing seller", but you have to know enough to decide how much you're prepared to pay.'*
>
> DAVID COAN

THE TECHNOLOGICAL AGE

The major technologies that have become essential to our day-to-day lives are to do with appliances, transport, communication and media. Yet technology isn't only about the bare necessities, it also enriches our culture and can give great pleasure. From tin toys to robots to mechanical musical instruments, some of the intriguing machines that have been shown on *Collectors' Lot* were made purely to entertain.

Since the beginning of the twentieth century, life has moved at a faster pace. Technology has not only provided us with time-saving gadgets, it has also helped speed things up. Now there's always more to see and do, and longer distances to travel.

Until recently, the relics of our industrial past – domestic and professional working tools – haven't been high on the list of most collectors. Old irons, lawnmowers and steam engines routinely went on the scrap heap – but that seems to be changing. Today, there are a growing number of collectors who treasure these poor relations of the collecting world for what they tell us about the way that society has developed.

Other technologies have been widely collected for many years so the markets are well established and items can cost a fortune. These are usually things that can boast a long history of aesthetic as well as mechanical design. Some are old and precious enough to be classed as true 'antiques' rather than 'collectables'. A quality watch can inspire the same sense of awe in a horologist as a Rolls Royce does for some vintage car enthusiasts. Yet, for a fairly modest sum, it's possible to build up a worthwhile collection in these areas.

It isn't unusual to find an optician who collects spectacles, a doctor who collects medical instruments, a television technician who collects televisions or a programmer who collects computers. Equally, though, an interest could be sparked by a strong childhood memory or a pure appreciation of mechanics.

As far as current or recent technology is concerned, prices vary enormously at the moment and it is difficult to predict which buys will make sound investments. Generally, however, it's often the things that were less successful in their day, and therefore made in small numbers, that attract a good price later on. Also, the first examples of a particular technology – an early personal computer or mobile phone, for instance – are always sought after. Collectors will look at the design as well as the innards, but if they want it then the only deterrent in this collecting area is likely to be lack of storage space.

This 1950s pocket watch is similar in design to the railway pieces of the nineteenth century. Watches made at this time were the last remnants of the English horology industry.

TECHNOLOGY IN THE HOME

Here we are, at the end of a century, having done the shopping and the laundry, mown the lawn, hoovered the house, phoned a few friends and cooked dinner. Maybe later we'll have a shower, turn up the heating and curl up to watch the television or surf the net. We take for granted the technology that has altered the way we live, but it's a far cry from the time when a battery of servants were hired simply to run the household, to keep it warm and do the chores.

Among the jobs a maid would have done was to light fires in the bedrooms and pour hot water into a wash-jug. Yet, piped hot and cold water had been technically available since the 1820s. Even in grand households, it seems, the idea of a bathroom was slow to catch on, because people preferred the warmth of the bedroom for washing. So, availability of a technology alone isn't enough to guarantee its success – practicalities such as money and culture are important, too.

It's stunning to think how slow some useful inventions have been to catch on. Electrical appliances, for example, have been available from the 1890s. Yet it was to be over forty years before they became commonly available. Electrical engineer and collector Colin Hill has been buying up old electrical appliances, dead or alive, for years. He became interested after delving into social history when he was working for the electricity board.

'One lady I met had electricity installed in 1910 and I asked her if she thought it was a good thing,' says Colin. ' "Oh yes, wonderful," the lady said, "I could turn on the electric light to find the matches to light the gas!"'

Unlike modern irons, there are no controls of any kind on this early electric iron (it dates from around 1900). The plug would be removed from the socket when the clothes began to burn. Because of its simple design, the iron is still in working order after almost 100 years.

Convenience didn't come cheap. The first electric kettles weren't very successful. The few who could afford them weren't convinced it was safe to mix water, metal and electricity. Also, the kitchen range provided a constant source of heat, which was a highly efficient way of boiling up large quantities of water. In fact, it wasn't until the 1930s that the public became more keen to use electrical appliances, and even then they were mainly for lighting and ironing. People had good reason to be cautious: many old appliances were dangerous by our standards. With the advent of the national grid, the supply of electricity became safer and more reliable and prices of appliances started to fall.

ELECTRICAL APPLIANCES
Colin Hill

'I have an interest in the history of electrical technology,' says Colin Hill, whose collection of electrical appliances dates from 1890 to around 1950. 'You can't separate the technology from the people who used it. And in appliances you can see the developments of style from Art Nouveau through to Art Deco. For example, the casing of an electric fire element would take on the colours and shapes of the period of manufacture. Early appliances used traditional materials, like cast iron, brass, wood and copper. Later, plastics and aluminium were introduced. You can see the techniques too, which developed from the use of nuts and bolts through to pressed and moulded parts.

Ronning bootwarmers of the 1940s. A good idea, but like most appliances of the period, not very safe.

'The best places to buy are second-hand markets, but items may be scruffy, with missing parts – I like to restore things. Plugs were all different before the 1930s, so it's not merely the parts that I have to find but vintage plugs and cables as well. These have usually been cut off and thrown away. You couldn't move things from one house to another in that period without buying new plugs.

'One of the rarest items in my collection is an early electric Dowsing tube type of fire – they were only made from 1896 to about 1915. I found it in a junk shop in very bad condition. When I was on *Collectors' Lot* I got a few parts sent to me and I've restored it to its former glory, which has given me great pleasure.

'Collecting is something that catches you unawares. I have to be choosy about what I buy now as there's a limit to how many electric appliances you can store in a bungalow. (My limit is much higher than my wife's!)'

This 'Lincoln' fire made by His Master's Voice in the 1950s is remarkable for its 'American auto' styling. It was an effective heater that used aluminium reflectors.

Vacuum Cleaners

David Dunning

'VACUUM CLEANERS ARE A BIT LIKE CARS, but cheaper,' says David Dunning, a presenter on Radio York, who started with a pink Constellation – and never looked back.

'I find hoarding is a great way of keeping in touch with the past. I'm certainly not a minimalist person! But I also love the process of slimming collections down now and again.

'Collecting vacuum cleaners happened by accident about ten years ago. I needed one to

Part of David's collection of vacuum cleaners, most of which he keeps in the loft. Although he has around sixty cleaners, David hates hoovering. His collection does earn its keep, however, by helping to publicise his radio show.

use, so I went to a second-hand shop and found one for £30. It still works, but I kept finding others I liked. I've got about sixty altogether, they're mostly stored in the loft

The Constellation captured the public's imagination. With its space-age appearance, it seemed to follow you around the room.

now. I actually *use* a modern micro-cylinder thing, which is lightweight. Unfortunately, I have cats and a dark green carpet that shows everything and I hate vacuuming.

'As a kid, I remember the latest fashion was the Hoover Constellation. It was like a big round blob, made of metal, that floated on its own output a bit like a hovercraft. Switched off it was quite heavy, but once powered up you could move it with a finger. At the time it was linked to the space race, a typical early 1960s innovation. I've got one on display. It matches the pink carpet on my landing, which was left behind by the previous owners.

'I like the social history behind vacuum cleaners and I buy because the design appeals. The best designs were from Hoover when it reigned supreme up to the 1970s.

'My collection has attracted lots of coverage on national television and radio and in the press, which helps to publicise Radio York. This means the vacuum cleaners have made me rather famous, or is that infamous…?

'I don't actually know what to do with them. I believe they'll have a value one day. Sometimes I imagine what it would be like if I gave them away, but I take some pleasure in thinking what a problem they'll be to sort out after I die! I've got a little nephew called Rhys who likes them – he might want them one day.'

COLLECTING VACUUM CLEANERS

Anyone who saw commercial television in its earliest days would remember the advertisement – 'Hoover beats as it sweeps as it cleans'. The term 'hoovering' came from the Hoover company, which designed vacuum cleaners from 1908. They were welcomed from the 1920s, when they were imported from the US. They were one of the first appliances to be sold door-to-door on hire purchase agreements and could be 'traded in' for a fresh buy. They sold well during the 1950s, when people had more money to spend on 'luxuries'.

Before vacuum cleaners, rugs and carpets were hung on the washing line and beaten to get the dust out. The earliest examples, patented in 1901 in Britain, were powered by a petrol engine and pulled along on a horse drawn contraption that you hired at great cost. The first domestic Hoovers were hand operated, pump-action ones. These were featured in the television series *Upstairs, Downstairs*.

Finding Hoovers in a good condition is hard, as they take a battering. Prices are low for all but those in good or mint condition.

Vacuum cleaners have become much lighter over the years.

NEW COMMUNICATIONS TECHNOLOGY

News has never travelled faster than it does today. We hear about events at the other side of the world almost in real time. People don't only watch and listen, but record, photograph and film events on domestic machines. 'Communications technology', covers a gamut of subjects including radio, television, film, photography, computing and telecommunications. Many of them were in their infancy in the nineteenth century and evolved throughout the twentieth century. With the coming of the age of digital they are changing again.

Collectors learn to recognise the age and quality of an item from its design and the materials it is made from. Some choose to focus on one obscure area. Peter Bowgett, for example, collects television test cards. He's made it his quest to find each one and make a record for posterity. Another speciality item is the phonecard, available in ever-changing designs and now a popular collectable, widely traded between enthusiasts.

Other collections are more eclectic. Michael Bennett-Levy, of the parts shop Early Technology in Edinburgh is a collector turned dealer, who is able to supply parts for restoring objects that might come loosely under the heading of early technology, from valves to microchips.

This is an area of vastly differing tastes, and only a collector can decide what is worth buying. Whoever would have thought, for example, that the humble Brownie 127 box camera would ever be a collectable? Cameras aren't the only photographic collectable: film, negatives, flash equipment, light meters, stereoscopes and all kinds of optical toys are also in demand.

Items produced when a technology was new are sought after. 'Very early televisions are recognisable by their small screens and big cabinets,' says collector, John Gillies. 'There are still bargains to be found in sets that were made before 1953, when they became more common as many people bought them to watch the coronation.'

If you are wondering whether to hold on to a piece of new technology, the golden rule is that anything that is a departure from the norm, whether ultimately successful or not, is likely to be attractive to collectors now or in the future.

Few of Clive Sinclair's inventions have enjoyed lasting commercial success, but some, such as the original Sinclair Spectrum, have begun to attract attention from collectors.

TELEVISION TEST CARDS
Peter Bowgett

Television test cards have been part of Peter Bowgett's life ever since he was a child. 'There was a time when the test card music played an important part,' says Peter, who lives in Lancashire. 'My parents had divorced and it seemed to add a sort of predictability and stability to life – that the 'Royal Daffodil' was always followed by, 'Lark in the Clear Air' then 'Asia Minor', and so on. I still like the instrumental music; but very little is commercially available these days.

'You don't often see television test cards today, but they were more familiar to viewers during the 1950s and 1960s, when programmes were limited to just a few hours a day and technicians needed to test how well sets performed against a standard picture. Then the music was added to make television sets more attractive in salesrooms.

'I'd never collected anything before, but I used to come across pictures in television repair books. There was never any information about them and I became intrigued by why Test Card D replaced Test Card C and so on.'

So Peter set out to solve the mystery. The result was that, with the help of fellow enthusiasts and the BBC archives, several years later he had gathered a collection of almost all the test cards used by the BBC and ITA from 1946 to the present day, and is completing a book about them that will be the definitive work. Peter also collects television sets for erecting displays to provide illustrations for the book.

'Originals are nice to have, but that's not my fascination, it's more the intellectual challenge of piecing it all together.' The music is proving more tricky, but he's managed to collect over a hundred cassettes, open reels, CDs and minidiscs, and along the way has met a few friends who are also test card enthusiasts.

'Test cards have never been a complete life absorption. I work on the book when I have the time, usually during the winter. Once the book's finished I was thinking of going into Amateur TV, I'll sit in front of camera and transmit, a sort of CBTV. Of course it would have to have test cards in it.'

COLLECTOR'S TIP

'The internet is a good way to contact collectors with a similar interest, but it's best to meet face to face to exchange or buy.'

CHARLIE LOCKWOOD

Phonecard Collectors' Club

Cameras
David Coan

'I LIKE ALL THINGS MECHANICAL, but steam engines are too big to collect,' says David Coan of Chorley in Lancashire. Instead he opted for a collection of cameras and then proceeded to amass possibly the largest personal collection in the north-west.

'Collecting cameras is a passion with me. Now I'm retired I spend as much time documenting and researching as collecting.

'In the 1970s, I started collecting anything that came to hand. I began to read books about cameras and bought them, although I was more restricted, having a mortgage and young children. Before long my wife started to complain about my collection taking over the wardrobe, so I moved them to the loft. Since we moved house, I keep the collection more securely.

David's enormous collection of cameras includes some that he has lusted after since he was a young man. He brings out examples to talk to photographic societies and other groups.

'You become more knowledgeable and refine your tastes over time. Once you've got over 1,100, you don't often find something you want that you haven't already got.

'Different collectors have different motivations. For me, it's the mechanics and the visual attraction. I don't specialise, although I enjoy collecting bizarre cameras and asking, "Why on earth did they design it like that?" '

COLLECTING CAMERAS

A box with a lens that focused light on to an inside surface was invented around 1650, but it wasn't until the photographic system was invented in the 1830s that a camera was able to produce a permanent image.

The earliest and the most valuable cameras are the wet plate cameras of 1840–80. These have a silver wire inside the plate carrier. Manufacturers' names and patent numbers are often a clue to date. These rare cameras are admired for their craftsmanship. All-wood cameras of two concentric sliding boxes are more desirable than the rarer bellows version.

Eastman's development of the dry plate in 1879 led to the mass production of cameras. Collectors are drawn to the quality of workmanship and materials rather than to technical features.

The British camera industry was active up to the 1950s. It suffered when good quality imports became available from Germany, Japan, Hong Kong and Russia.

Age is not a predictor of value. Early Edwardian can cost less than 1950s cameras. Bargains can often be found at jumble or car boot sales.

Brass-and-mahogany cameras are highly collectable.

TIMEPIECES

Time features heavily in most people's lives these days. How long a task or journey takes, how fast something goes. Few people are without a watch of some sort. Measuring and displaying time accurately happened with the invention of clocks and watches. The earliest clock is the one at Salisbury Cathedral, believed to have been made in the fourteenth century. But it took another 350 years to produce the first personal pocket watch.

Timepieces, both old and new, are valued as much for their decorative appeal as for their technology. The style, the mechanism and the material it's made from are what gives the clock or watch its value.

The gentleman's pocket watch on the left is of sterling silver and dates from 1911. The fobwatch on the right would have been worn by a lady as a pendant or brooch. It has an 18-carat gold case, inner case and dial.

Though it is sometimes expensive (a collector paid £192,000 for a rare Patek Philippe wristwatch a few years ago), a collectable watch can cost just a few pounds. It depends what league you decide to play in.

Generally speaking, women's wristwatches tend to cost less than men's and are collected more as pieces of jewellery than for their mechanisms. The big money is paid for men's watches, which are valued as status symbols in certain circles. At this level, people need to be aware of the fakes of some expensive watches. They're not difficult to spot for someone experienced in handling them: they're generally lighter and made from cheap materials. At the highest level, watch collecting is a specialist skill with international appeal – a few people fly across oceans to buy a special and rare timepiece.

'Timex or Rolex, it doesn't matter to me, they're equally interesting in different ways,' says Kim-John Webb, the horologist who appeared on *Collectors' Lot.*

Premier league watches include Patek Philippe, Cartier, the International Watch Company, Jaeger-LeCoultre, Rolex and Vacheron Constantin. First league items are Chopard, Movado, Omega, Longine, Piaget and Seiko (Japan). They will probably cost more than Bulova, Baume & Mercier, Ingersoll, Raymond Weil, Rotary, Timex and Tissot.

Prices can be volatile, so before you spend a large amount, it's best to find out more from specialist publications, like *Watch.*

COLLECTING SWATCHES
Stanford Moseley

'Collecting, to me, is about having fun, getting nice things,' says Stanford Moseley, an aerobics instructor and chef from Bristol, who collects Swatches, the technology that revived the Swiss watch industry.

'I've always liked watches and buying a Swatch is a way of adding an accessory to your wardrobe, without it being too expensive. Knowing the time isn't important – you wear a nice pair of trousers and a watch to match. I don't take it too seriously, but if I'm in funky club clothing I don't want to be wearing Cartier.

'My style is modern: le Corbusier, pop-art, Art Deco, modern studio pottery. Things don't have to have a monetary value, but I don't like tat. I'd never wear a watch out of my collection unless I had two of them. I probably wear about fifteen out of the 600 or so I've got.

'The "specials" are the most fantastic part. If you can get one at a reasonable price, you've got a piece of artwork. Four of the Swatches were designed by the artist Keith Haring; only 1,000 were released, at around $35 each. Now one would cost around £1,000.

'A Swatch is a laser sealed watch. You can't get into the casing. If it goes wrong it's dead. The idea was that you needn't worry about losing it but trying to replace the old ones from the 1980s is difficult. Early designs like the "black-out" or the "tennis grid" or the "jellyfish" (first see-through watch) would cost a lot more now. The "tennis grid" was particularly vile.'

Swatches were first brought out in 1983. They were an immediate success because they offered new technology and novel designs at reasonable prices. Collectors look for 1980s models, particularly the 'specials', which were designed by well known artists. The most desirable Swatches are unworn and are still in their original unopened bubble packs. The earliest models, from the first two collections, have seven holes in the strap and should still have their guarantee which, somewhere, will carry the date.

CARING FOR WATCHES

- Always take valuable watches to a respected watchmaker for repairs.
- Most early watches are not waterproof, so do not get them wet.
- Do not over wind watches as this will damage or break the spring.
- Before spending a lot of money on a watch, check that the mechanism is original.
- Novelty watches, such as Swatches, will be worth more if they are in their original packaging.

Watches and Clocks

Kim-John Webb

'SOME PEOPLE CAN BE A BIT PRISSY about their subjects; if I can get them to come down from their ivory towers and give the information to the man in the street, I'll be happy,' so says Kim-John Webb, professional horologist and collector of everything to do with watches and clocks.

'I've got clocks, pocket watches, wrist watches, tools and so on. I love them because they live; they have a heartbeat, which is the mechanism. Appearance is the starting point; how good something looks, or its unusualness. For example I found a big silver-case pocket watch recently. It was obviously too heavy to carry, but I thought it might have been designed to put into a saddle. It's got nothing about it aesthetically, but the substantiality of the item compelled me to look inside it.

'I'm lucky having the watch repair side for my business. I'd never played with a watch until I came into the trade, then it was the diversity that interested me. No two mechanisms seem to be the same, especially before 1850. Even modern things are cased or dialled differently. Customers realise I'm interested and come in to show me things. The collecting expands my knowledge, which makes me a better repairer, and vice versa.

'For me the collecting represents a constant quest for knowledge. Now I know so much about mechanisms, I find my interest in history is developing. I'm learning fine art evaluation, to see how the development of some things affects others. You can see how, from the earliest watches around 1650–80 in Britain we influenced the continent. After

that, the continent took it up and improved on what we'd started.

'I don't ever buy to invest, but the social life is important. Like most other watch collectors I'm interested in other people's collections, and find them educational. My main problem is security, which is why I don't show the collection very often and why I don't keep it in an obvious place.

'Watches are my life. I'm a Muppet, a sad person whose life is boring to other people because of my watches. I try not to talk about it unless someone asks me, and I have got other interests! I've got my amateur thespian activities, I sing and dance and do kung fu, so horology isn't everything.

'If I was buying a watch that didn't work, in the hope it could be repaired, I'd see if I could get it to tick in all positions. If it does, that tells you the balance staff is working, which is an expensive thing to replace. If it has an enamel dial, check there are no cracks in it. If you're going to pay as much as £40 you'd want a perfect dial.'

The mechanism of this pocket watch, made around 1900, has many high class features.

Kim-John Webb collects all kinds of timepieces and related memorabilia. He is seen here in front of a mid-eighteenth century longcase clock, wearing a pocket watch and Albert chain of similar age. The chains get their name from Queen Victoria's husband, who made them fashionable.

COLLECTING WATCHES AND CLOCKS

Early pocket watches, made from 1670 through the eighteenth century, would have belonged to the gentry. They're rare and expensive now. They became smaller with increasing skill, so by the end of the nineteenth century discreet watches were the most expensive. Most of the pocket watches you'll find at collectors' fairs were made during the late Victorian and Edwardian periods.

One of the first wristwatches was made in 1908 for the daredevil Brazilian aviator, Alberto Santos-Dumont, by his jeweller friend Louis Cartier. Cartier still makes the 'Santos' today, as a collector's piece.

The wristwatches issued to the armed forces were the first to be mass produced to a consistent quality. You might pick up a broken watch for £10, but it might cost up to £100 to repair – if it's repairable.

NOVELTY CLOCKS AND MECHANICAL MUSIC

Technology has been used to provide entertainment as well as to further industry. Mechanical musical instruments have delighted people since Victorian times. The first musical box was made in 1796 in Switzerland. The forerunner was the carillon in town hall towers, which was a series of different bells playing a tune dictated by pins on a cylinder. The great era for musical box collectors is 1850–1900, and it is still possible to find mid-Victorian examples at auction – for a price.

The twentieth century's novelties are still available and are sometimes not too expensive, particularly if something is in a sorry state and in need of repair. Usually, the advice is to find a professional restorer, but for many collectors the attraction is in finding

Roman Piekarski in his cuckoo clock museum. He and his brother have now started to collect fairground organs by the same makers.

CUCKOO CLOCKS
Roman Piekarski

'The greatest part is the hunt. You get a sniff of something, follow it up and go in for the kill.' Roman Piekarski and his brother Maz have over 500 cuckoo clocks in their museum at Tabley, Cheshire. They remember growing up with a cuckoo clock in the family home because their parents loved them.

'We bought our first cuckoo clock at an antique market twenty-five years ago. We call it the acorn from which the oak has grown. Since then I've put all my energy into building the collection. I enjoy the look on people's faces when they see them all.

It gives us an excuse to keep going back to the Black Forest, where we can continue our never ending research. We've recently started collecting and restoring fairground organs made by the same people. They're quite spectacular but the clocks will always be my one true love.'

MUSIC MACHINES
Graham Whitehead

'When I was six I went to see a Laurel and Hardy film and remember being particularly impressed by the pianola,' says Graham Whitehead of Ashorne, near Warwick. Now he owns a house large enough to display and repair mechanical musical machines. When I left school, I accepted a job as a cinema projectionist in Coventry. The first sound I heard on my first day at work was the song "In a Monastery Garden" played on the cinema organ. Every week the films would change, but the organ remained the same.

'I wanted to be a cinema engineer, but in the 1950s cinema seemed doomed, so I found a job in the print industry.

'I started collecting mechanical musical instruments in 1970, when I bought a modern musical box in Switzerland. I now have about sixty pieces, ranging from musical boxes as small as tea caddies to a huge dance organ 27 ft (8 m) long and 16 ft (5 m) wide. The centrepiece is a cinema organ, housed in the ballroom of Ashorne Hall, once a semi-derelict building, which has been restored over the last seven years.

'Nine months ago I left the print industry to make a career out of my hobby. The music machines are so cheerful and such a good reminder of a bygone age. Instead of watching television my wife Janet and I often sit in our music room and play music rolls on our Ampico "reproducing" grand piano.'

COLLECTOR'S TIP

'When repairing mechanisms, be aware of your own limitations and don't ruin a potentially valuable piece.'

KIM-JOHN WEBB

out how an object works and returning it to its former glory. That involves both mechanics and aesthetics.

Cuckoo clocks have been a traditional cottage industry since around 1700. Most of the world's cuckoo clocks have been made within the Black Forest region of Germany, where they are still made today. Early mechanisms were made out of seasoned beech (today they are metal), and the hands and numerals were often bone and antler. Two small whistles in the clock produced the familiar 'cuck-oo' sound. The mechanisms of some of the older clocks are beautifully made, but due to the use of automata they are easily thrown off balance, so collectors need to find a specialist restorer, such as Roman Piekarski.

COLLECTOR'S TIP

'Look out for things of special interest in small general auctions. These are where you might find a bargain.'

TRAVEL

Public and personal transport was one of the spin-offs of the Industrial Revolution. Old cars, planes, trams and trains evoke great nostalgia these days, so it's no wonder that collecting the paraphernalia of transport has become an absorbing hobby for thousands. Railway lamps, nameplates or badges, bus tickets and even aircraft sickbags, are just a few of the collections that have been featured on *Collectors' Lot*. There are people who collect cars and even real trains, too.

The first car, known as a 'horseless carriage', was just that – a carriage with an engine underneath. It crawled along the streets in the late nineteenth century, frightening pedestrians and horses alike. By 1910, however, cars were beginning to look a bit more like the cars we know today, with a front engine, a bonnet and a boot. It wasn't long before the motor car was racing along country lanes as if it had a mind of its own.

Of course cars, trains and planes – not forgetting the spectacular hot air balloons that, from 1783, gave a lucky few their first bird's eye view of the world – are not practical collectables for most people. Happily, we can see them in museums or exhibitions around the country. Transport collectables on a less grand scale are another matter. Some of the luxurious accessories, car coats and helmets or silver mascots are highly collectable now. The cost will depend on the condition, materials and design, and as always, how many people want them.

One of the most vigorous collecting areas is trains and train memorabilia. Gerald Baker has specialised by collecting printed material related to the Great Western Railway (GWR). Even so, he has found that there is a lot of 'cross-over' with other collecting areas and he has to compete with general railway collectors, specialist dealers and auction houses. Over one million GWR jigsaws were made with Chad Valley from 1942 – the first of forty-three titles was Caerphilly Castle – but these all attract attention from the toy market. Likewise GWR posters, especially those from the 1930s, are popular with poster collectors.

Keith Seume, who collects VW Beetles, has had less trouble finding literature about his field, perhaps because car owners tend to keep their manuals. If you are interested in beginning or adding to a collection of travel memorabilia, then you could attend the travel auctions at Christie's or Onslow's in London. There are also specialist book and travel shops or, like collector Mike Smith, you could visit the autojumbles advertised in car magazines.

GWR MEMORABILIA
Gerald Baker

'Some fifteen years ago I stumbled across a book, *Go Great Western*, which charts the history of publicity associated with Great Western Railway. From then on, I have collected anything to do with GWR, including booklets, brochures, posters and jigsaw puzzles.' Gerald Baker tells how he has amassed over 500 items of GWR printed material.

'I've always had an interest in the great Victorian engineer Isambard Kingdom Brunel, who was responsible for building ships, like the *Great Western*, and bridges–such as the Clifton Suspension Bridge – and the Great Western Railway, which terminated in Bristol. Seeing a Brunel ship, the SS *Great Britain*, brought back to Bristol from the Falklands was another thing that fired my interest.

'Although it's a fairly narrow subject, it's still sociable. I meet fellow collectors at specialist sales and auctions, but many I've grown to know over the phone.

'My favourite item is a jigsaw puzzle made one Christmas in the 1930s for the employees at GWR's Swindon works. Very few of the jigsaws survived.'

The first book for the traveller was published in 1904. *The Cornish Riviera* by A. M. Broadley sold over 250,000 copies at 3d each and remained in print for twenty years. Other books followed, as well as booklets and brochures for the travelling public. There were books on fishing, rambling and camping, books about famous trains such as *The Cheltenham Flyer* and *The 10.30 Limited*, a Heath Robinson cartoon book, works on castles, abbeys and cathedrals on the line, and handbooks for travellers from overseas.

Holiday Haunts ran for over forty years from 1906 to 1947, first at 3d a copy, then at 6d from 1911.

Various books and brochures describing the delights of the Cornish, Devon and Somerset coastlines, which could be accessed from the GWR.

AUTOMOBILIA
Mike Smith

'The sort of things that attract me are those which no-one ever imagined would be collectable – oil pumps, road signs, badges and mascots.' For twenty-two years Mike Smith's passion has been automobilia and his garage in Buckinghamshire is a tribute to the motoring age of the past.

'One of the most interesting features of my collection is the reconstruction of an office, which could have been found in a country garage before World War II. In those days garages provided a great variety of services. If you ran out of lamp oil, or needed your lawnmower repaired you'd go to your local garage. Every village had one.

'You don't need a great expanse of space for automobilia, and it needn't cost you a fortune. For example, people are still discarding old petrol pumps. You just have to keep your eyes and ears open. Restoration is not difficult, but it takes time and to buy a fully restored pump would be expensive.

'I go to autojumbles somewhere every week. I've made automobilia my business now, but my collection is quite separate, nothing in it is for sale.'

Mike has reconstructed a typical pre-war country garage. The breadth of the services available at the garage can be seen by the signs advertising spare parts, petrol, oil and other necessities hanging from the ceiling.

VOLKSWAGEN BEETLES
Keith Seume

'My brother discovered Beetles when he went to university in the late 1960s. I was just fourteen and became hooked, infatuated with everything to do with Beetles.' Keith Seume tells how meeting an extraordinary vehicle at an impressionable age, dictated his future.

'I hated the Mini, which was all I could afford as my first car. Eventually, I saved up enough for my first of thirty Beetles – a 1962 model that I bought in 1974.

'Later I began collecting literature, especially material supplied to VW dealers in the 1950s and 1960s. Happily, people tend not to throw things away. So when dealerships close down, bundles of spares and paperwork are on offer. The walls of my office are lined with it. I can look at it as research material, but it's quite valuable in itself as VW is a "mature" collectors' market.

'You could say my hobby has become all-absorbing. I launched the magazine *VolksWorld* in 1987, and my wife Gwynn – who was interested in VWs before she met me – runs her own mail-order business buying and selling modern VW collectable items.

'Our most cherished vehicle, out of seven, is a fully restored 1951 Beetle which we "show" at *concours* (short for *concours d'elegance*). Beetle owners bring their cars from all over the world to these gatherings, in England, France and Germany.'

If you're interested in collecting Beetle memorabilia, choose one specific area and concentrate on it. There's a lot of material out there. For example, if you choose to collect sales brochures from the 1960s, then there are probably 200 or more examples and translations in different languages. These would start from around £2–£3 each. Rarer brochures from the 1950s go for around £100, particularly those with beautifully stylised illustrations by an artist called Reuters.

The Beetle was sixty years old in 1998. To date, 22 million cars have been sold worldwide, and it is still being produced in Mexico. The Guinness Book of Records lists a 1963 Beetle as the most reliable car – it reached a mileage of 1,605,505.

COLLECTOR'S TIP

'*Automobilia events are listed in magazines such as* Classic Car Monthly *and the* Autojumblers Association *supplies information about dates and locations.*'

KEITH SEUME

CHAPTER SEVEN

In Print

Printed Material

Fewer items tell us more about how life has changed during the twentieth century than the words and images on printed collectables. They're appreciated for both their aesthetic qualities and for their content, which can reveal so much about the evolving values of past generations.

In the information age, it's hard to imagine there was ever a time without junk mail or the Sunday papers. We've grown accustomed to colourful billboards, too, and there aren't many products that are sold without their own distinctive brand packaging. The consumer society we take so much for granted began, by and large, around the middle of the nineteenth century. Many forces spurred it on, but one of the main ones was that printing and publishing techniques improved.

Old books, leaflets and magazines give a collector hours of entertainment and a valuable insight into past lives. Smaller items too, hold the attention, because all printed collectables have an ephemeral quality. The century can be traced through cereal packets, birthday cards or bus tickets. Many are worth very little in monetary terms, their value is in their nostalgia, but occasionally a rare scrap or a postcard will fetch a small fortune at auction. All this means rich pickings and lots of fun for collectors, who have a knack of looking at the ordinary in an extraordinary way.

COLLECTOR'S TIP

'Dealers are generous with information. A lot of them are collectors and dealing is only a sideline.'

DAVID COX

128

GETTING INTO PRINT

Story telling and the passing on of information was almost all by word of mouth in villages at the start of the nineteenth century. Very few families could read or write and books were expensive luxuries. Paper was handmade from recycled linen or cotton, bindings had to be sewn or laced to stiff outer boards, and colour had to be painted by hand on to black-and-white prints.

By the end of that century, developments in printing techniques had transformed the industry. Most spectacular was the invention of colour printing, or chromolithography, in the late 1830s. The technique was used to produce quality colour plates in books, copies of popular paintings, greetings cards and packaging.

Children waited with baited breath each week to see what the heroes and villains in the Eagle, *the* Lion *or the* Champion *had got up to. The above comics date from the 1950s and 1960s.*

Another technique that had earlier been used on pottery, transfer printing, was adapted for use on tins. Until then, colour printing hadn't been successful on tins because chromolithography required an absorbent surface. No-one is quite certain exactly when transfer printing on to tins was introduced here, but in the 1860s British printers were corresponding with the French about it.

Social change, too, encouraged the market for attractive colour printing. Primary education was compulsory from the 1870s, so children learned to read and books became more common. By the start of the twentieth century, most people made or bought cards at Christmas, sent postcards from resorts and read a magazine or newspaper when they could afford it. In their homes people hung framed colour prints on the parlour walls.

The introduction of photolithography in the 1920s made colour printing faster and easier, although the quality of reproduction suffered. In the 1960s new photographic techniques changed the processes further, then in the 1980s computer technology brought a new dimension to print as it did to other industries. Not only has the nature of printing and publication changed, but also many of the traditional skills have been replaced by new methods.

PRINTED EPHEMERA AND POSTCARDS

Though a lot of effort was put into producing them, it was the destiny of printed ephemera to be thrown away. Yet enough has survived to give collectors the fun of rooting it out. All printed materials are potentially collectable: postcards, cigarette cards, old photographs, bubble gum wrappers, sheet music, menu cards, greetings cards, magazines, tickets or shop counter displays. In fact anything printed on paper or card which isn't made to last. Look out, too, for the scraps that were designed so that people could use them to make up pictures, collages or cards. Some of the earliest, from the 1850s can be quite valuable; stickers would be their modern equivalent today.

The joy is that, for the most part, these paper items cost so little. If needs must, a collection can be built simply by retrieving things from the bin. This 'rubbish' doesn't look so extraordinary right now, but in ten years time it'll be showing its age and will be telling a story, and may even acquire some monetary, as well as nostalgic value. The main attractions, though, are older items.

When assessing value, there are two main criteria. The first is to do with condition, the other is rarity. Lots of people, for example, kept their wartime ration books, so these will cost very little, a pound or two. 'Special issue' magazines, which commemorate certain events, such as the coronation, can be bought from a couple of pounds and may just about creep up into double figures for less common editions at specialist collectors fairs. But rare items marking events that have grown in significance are valuable. For instance, a timetable listing South Eastern Railway's trips to Paris in the 1860s may cost around £80. Similarly, an old copy of the *Beano* would cost very little, but the rare first edition is worth around £1,000, according to price guides.

This discrepancy in price can be confusing, but it's all part of the challenge. As with all collecting areas an item is worth what a collector is willing to pay. All things considered, the attraction of collecting something so plentiful is that you're not likely to become frustrated by the rarity of an item for quite some time. Only after exploring what's available and what's scarce should you start spending larger amounts.

The first British picture postcard with a date stamp was sent in 1894. It was a view of Scarborough, not so different to the ones that you find in any seaside town today. Individually, postcards are rarely of great value – most old cards can be bought for less than £5 each and often only pence. Landscapes and architecture are

POSTCARDS
Stella Blazier

'They are lovely, they cheer me up. I keep thinking I must have them all by now, but they keep turning up,' says Stella Blazier, who has collected over 1,300 postcards of twins since her daughters were born twenty-one years ago.

'I like the funny ones, with clever puns, like "We called the second one encore, he wasn't in the original programme." Women had no way of knowing for sure, so the jokes cover up what could have been a traumatic event. The cards provide us with a snapshot of social and domestic history; the messages on the back, another more personal cameo.

'When the girls were small, it was quite a big thing to get out to collectors' fairs. More recently I've given one or two talks to the National Women's Register, and written a book with a few friends.

'I think that there's a tremendous wave of nostalgia at the moment. It's the first time we've had so much disposable income – there didn't used to be money to spend on bits of cardboard. I haven't got vast resources to spend on my hobby, I seldom pay more than two or three pounds. I didn't think my collection would grow to such proportions.'

Arithmetic cards such as One and One Makes Three (left) *were very popular.* Do You Like Dancing? (right) *dates from 1914. It is one of many cards to contain a pun.*

usually considered too ordinary. You'll pay more for something out of the ordinary – military, transport, heraldry and political propaganda and some cartoons, such as those by Victorian artist Louis Wain, or the Donald McGill 1950s ones featuring red cheeked policeman, busty women and weedy men. Postcards are more expensive in sets, such as a set of 1930s sportsmen. A card posted to mark a significant event (the first cross channel flight for example), will command a high price, as will one with a rare postmark, such as a World War I card sent from the battle zone. There are plenty more special ones for £10 or so at postcard fairs, expect to pay between £25 and £50 for exceptionally scarce postcards. There are many clubs run by enthusiasts, and some excellent magazines, such as *Picture Postcard Monthly*.

As far as photographs are concerned, with Victorian images the main interest is in their technical rather than their artistic merit. Later, the subject, photographer and the image's aesthetic qualities are paramount. A collector has to bear in mind, however, that the provenance is often difficult to establish. Many fakes are now known. Pictures of famous subjects are collectable, but the price will reflect the quantity of prints in circulation and the age of the print: new prints from old negatives are of less interest. The work of top notch photographers now goes for thousands. For lesser prints expect to pay anything from 50p to £300–£400.

The quality of a Victorian photograph is usually judged on technical merit, unless the subject is extra-ordinary, as in this image of a Mazawattee tea cart being pulled by zebras.

CIGARETTE CARDS
John Walton

'As soon as I saw them I knew that cigarette cards were what I wanted to collect.' says John Walton, of the Cartophilic Society.

'I suppose I was going back to boyhood. I had an uncle who collected them, I remember he had a set of the pre-war cricketers. At the moment I'm trying to complete my own set of Taddy's county cricketers. There are 238 altogether, issued around 1908. I need about twenty-five, but they're mostly in the hands of dealers and can cost over £20 each.

'I think I'm probably typical of the people who've been collecting quite a while. More recent collectors, probably because of the cost of the cards nowadays, will focus on a certain subject. In the old days you collected anything.

'I love older cards because of the lithographic printing, which was beautiful and fresh. The colours of the military uniforms, especially, have a great appeal for me. I love the beauty cards, too. The figures of actresses were completely different at the beginning of the century, they had real hour-glass shapes.'

Cards came with tea, bubble gum and other commodities as well as cigarettes, but the generic term is cigarette cards. The 1930s are thought of as 'modern', old is Victorian, through Edwardian up to the time of World War I. John explains, 'Pictures of movie stars were quite common in the 1930s. In recent years the catalogue price went up, but that's not always reflected in the demand. Some sets, which are cataloguing for £30, go for under £10 a set at conventions.'

These cards are from a set called Hints on Association Football, issued by Player's in the 1930s.

ADVERTISING AND PACKAGING

Since the development of colour printing in the 1830s, some of the best artists of each successive decade have designed for commercial companies. This means that there is a wide range of attention-grabbing packaging and advertising for collectors. These are things that give clues to the lifestyles of past generations. They transport us back in an instant, telling us what people valued, what they wanted to look like and how much things cost.

The distinctive lettering and pictures of particular brands is always interesting. Some are instantly recognisable and have hardly changed since they were first designed. Examples of this type of packaging include Colman's Mustard and Lyles Golden Syrup. Others, such as Rinso and Fry's Chocolate, seem to conjure up a bygone age. In years to come, maybe multinational brands, like Coca-Cola and McDonald's, will evoke the same nostalgia in children of today.

Run-of-the-mill advertising collectables can usually be found for less than £5 and often no more than a pound. As a general rule, people pay more for strong colours and striking design.

The more unusual items such as cardboard cut-outs or large display boxes that used to stand on the counters of a shop will normally cost between £5 and £20, though (as always) a few rarer items can command more. These latter items are usually the ones that look very familiar, but are difficult to find. For these, and more spectacular enamel signs, which can occasionally cost over £100, a specialist dealer is the most direct source, though you can expect the price to be a little higher.

There are many collecting clubs nationwide, both general societies and those for people who have a narrow collecting interest, such as philumeny, the study of matchbox labels or tryroemlophily, the study of Camembert cheese labels.

Licensing other companies to carry your logo is a good way of getting paid to advertise. These 'cans' are in fact cameras.

The golden era of tin making was from 1860 to 1940, and the colourful results are highly sought after today. What makes old tins so special is the way they evoke a time when life moved at a gentler pace. Romantic, perhaps, but much of the attention to detail that went into designing, printing and assembling tins was lost when modern printing methods were introduced in the 1920s. The use of photolithography meant that there were only a limited number of colours available.

Tins weren't made to last, though many have. Huntley & Palmers, the Reading biscuit makers, pioneered the use of printed tins for packaging provisions. To begin with, the tins were plain and had paper labels, and it wasn't until 1879 that the company were licensed to print directly on to tin. From then on a variety of novelty shaped tins evolved, including ones that resembled handbags, hearts and baskets. From the beginning of the twentieth century, shapes became more adventurous – tins that looked like bookshelves, trams, sentry boxes, trains or ships became collectors items.

People would save promotional coupons and send off for presentation tins, which they treasured and treated with care. A Christmas tin, in Edwardian homes, was an important symbol. Children collected souvenir tins even in those days, so you find them with bright colour printing, made into money boxes or in novelty shapes. Large tins were used to advertise products in stores at a time when there was no commercial television or radio.

Not all collectable tins are so decorative. An interesting collection can be built from the fairly ordinary containers used to hold general provisions. There was a time when every other home had an OXO tin or old tobacco tins, so there are a lot around. Once they were emptied, they were often used as containers for those small household necessities, such as buttons or screws.

Robert Opie, who appears regularly on *Collectors' Lot*, has traced the history of tinned packaging over the past century. His museum in Gloucester Docks is an inspiration to any collector. For those who want to buy, decorative tins can be expensive. It isn't unusual for rare novelty ones, from early in the century up to World War II, to cost £200–£300. Most prices won't be so prohibitive. You'll be able to buy attractive more recently made ones for only a few pounds.

CARING FOR TINS
- Never varnish tins as this discolours them.
- Dents can be eased out by stroking the inside gently with a wooden spoon.
- Rust can be removed from the inside with wire wool if it's not got a printed design.
- Remove rust on the outside by cleaning carefully with a non-abrasive liquid cleaner or metal polish. Dry thoroughly.

Mazawattee Tea

Diana James

Diana is shown here holding a copy of her book, The Story of Mazawattee Tea. *She is surrounded by company memorabilia, which she has gathered over the last twenty-five years. Her son, Stephen, will keep the collection going in years to come.*

'I THINK THERE'S A TOUCH OF MAGPIE blood in my veins,' says Diana James, who collects everything to do with 'Mazawattee' – the name that for a century meant a luscious cup of tea.

'My great-grandfather John Boon Densham founded the Mazawattee Tea Company in the 1860s. So I've got strong family reasons for collecting material produced by the company.

A tin made to hold Mazawattee tea.

'The name came from joining a Hindi word *Mazathe*, meaning luscious, and the Singhalese word *Wattee,* meaning garden or growth. The name fascinated the public and proved to be a great selling point. The company took a progressive attitude towards advertising, which helped to make the tea famous. It also means that there's a wealth of beautiful packaging to collect. There's a shop in Aldershot that still has an original Mazawattee ceiling – it's now a Post Office so anyone can go in and see it. 'My collection represents a social history of 1860–1960. It's amazing how far we've come. When my great-grandfather started there was no radio, and photography was in its infancy.

'I've written a book called *The Story of Mazawattee Tea.* My relatives were obviously a good source of information and I was able to make use of the extensive private family papers. I have now become more selective in my collecting and at present I am especially eager to get a "gas-proof" tea tin from the war years; and a cardboard box illustrated by Louis Wain of a dogs' regatta.

'Since my book was brought out, people are beating me to it in collecting related items; and prices have gone up. Some dealers have taken advantage, but others are still very reasonable. Making a collection like this can run away with the pounds.

'I think I'd have to be very old to give up collecting. In my case I can feel my ancestors pushing me on! And even after twenty-five years, there's always something unexpected. The first thing I collected was a blue enamel sign on a railway station. It was on the Tenterden line in Kent; one of the platforms was being dismantled.

'I suppose I'm typical of most collectors in that I like showing people what I've got and I'm flattered when I'm asked questions. Strangers write to me out of the blue, coming at the subject from all angles. I've recently heard from somebody whose grandma was a model for one of the advertisements.'

COLLECTING MAZAWATTEE TEA

The boom years of the Mazawattee Tea Company were from the late nineteenth to the early twentieth centuries, when production was based in a factory in New Cross, London. During this period a wealth of eye-catching packaging and advertisements was produced, which put the name on the lips of tea-drinkers across the country.

Cards of the kings and queens of England.

CARDS

Cards were important to well-heeled Victorians. They were often at the centre of an awesome system of etiquette. You couldn't leave your visiting card with just anyone. A family's fortune could rise or fall, a husband's business could be won or lost on the strength of a wife's 'visiting' skills. Luckily, wives unravelled these complicated friendship rituals by reading a whole range of etiquette books, printed from the nineteenth century up until the 1930s, when social changes made them less necessary. Successive editions of *Mrs Beeton's Book of Household Management* were indispensable to newly weds for over half a century.

Christmas cards and Valentines quickly became a popular tradition among the genteel classes after the introduction of the Penny Post in 1840. Queen Victoria used to send about a hundred Valentines every year, and ordinary people also sent them to friends and relatives. People had to be careful, though, because some designs had hidden meanings, for example, giving a lady a picture of a pair of gloves was hinting at a proposal.

From the late nineteenth century – thanks to the introduction of the Halfpenny Post and the rising standards of living – postcards and greetings cards at birthdays or Christmas, funeral cards and party invitations were exchanged and often put away as keepsakes. These expressions of care for friendships and good relations have continued throughout the twentieth century, although there have been spectacular changes in design.

There are still a lot of cards to be found from the 1920s right up to the present day, but the very old Victorian ones are getting more difficult to find. A great variety of materials were used in these, including paper lace, silk, embossed scraps, even shells. The best cards fold out, pop up or have moving parts. Towards the end of the nineteenth century, some were produced using celluloid, the earliest form of plastic. The most collectable, and the ones you have to pay the most for, are early examples of colour printing, cards with moving parts and those by the most famous designers, which can cost over £100.

Cards are not always very expensive. Some interesting if less spectacular ones can be found for around £5 or less. Once again, it's difficult for a beginner to gauge what constitutes a rare card – wherever possible get advice from an expert. Watch out, too, for reproductions. Old designs have been re-printed recently, and are sometimes passed off as old ones, though of course the smooth, modern paper is usually a giveaway.

VALENTINES
Judith Howard

Collector and long established dealer, Judith Howard, has been interested in Valentines since she found one that her grandfather had sent to her grandmother back in 1862. She has some useful advice for collectors.

'The fact is that though they look unique, Valentines were made in batches. In the nineteenth century there were paper lace machines that we don't see now. I've tried to make old style Valentines out of doilies, but they aren't intricate enough; the old ones were incredibly fine and detailed. What attracted me was that people could buy scraps and lacy bits, then put them together in an individual way. It's like looking in on people's lives, you get poems and personal messages. You feel it would be fun to find out what happened to people. Generally they were sent by the middle and upper classes.

'You can get wonderful chromolithographed cards by famous designers, such as Helena McGuire – famous for incredible animals – and the very pretty retro-style Kate Greenaway. In the middle of the nineteenth century there was a fashion for rude or insulting 'Penny Dreadfuls'. Among the most collectable are mechanical Valentines, which open out like little stages, and often have paper levers activating moving parts.

'You can still get ordinary ones cheaply that look pretty framed. You can buy better ones for £15–£20. The best can fetch over £100 and are usually found in auctions.'

Look and ask for Valentines at antique fairs, they're not always on display. Beware of reproductions, which the Americans started making to sell in museum shops. These are turning up at fairs, framed and sold as originals. It's best to buy cards unframed, then you can see what condition they're in and whether they open. It's fine to buy a card in poor condition, purely for

This Valentine was made in 1870 from paper lace and 'scrap'. The date of the paper was usually stamped on as a watermark. When held up to the light it is often visible.

David is seen here with a selection of cards dating from the 1860s to World War II. An early 3-D card showing a crib scene (back left) is behind a Christmas pudding card that opens to reveal a bottle of aromatic black draught to cure all ills. In the centre at the back are some early cards that feature Father Christmas.

Christmas Cards

David Cox

'LEAVE NO STONE UNTURNED. The dog that ferrets about finds the bone,' says David Cox, retired gardener of Cheltenham, who has a lifetime's collection of Victorian and Edwardian Christmas cards.

'After the war, my wife and I found some nice old Christmas cards. We were "shoe-string collectors" – and probably had a lot more fun than those who could just write a cheque for whatever they liked. In the 1950s and 1960s it was an absorbing hunt. There

were lots in junk shops and small antique shops or markets, and you could get very early ones.

'I've accumulated several hundred and what I like about them is that they're social objects, revealing of life as it was then through the class structure. They have a quite different interpretation of Christmas to the snow and robins of today. They show the class system, with the rich families going off to school and the urchins at the gate. The upper classes were

140

COLLECTING CHRISTMAS CARDS

The first Christmas cards came out in 1843, shortly after the Penny Post was introduced. Writer Sir Henry Cole suggested the idea to artist John Calcott Horsley. They became an annual event – just a thousand were printed in 1846 – and over the next fifty years cards swept the world. Typically the earliest showed sentimental scenes, with messages such as 'Sweet contentment, innocence and mirth, and good nature of the poor.' Not that the poor could have afforded them.

Many Victorians made their own cards using silks, ribbons, lace and pressed flowers. After 1870, when the Halfpenny Post was introduced, cards were mass produced and more affordable. You can still buy them for under £3, although you can pay £100 or more for some of the elaborate mechanical types of cards. Pop ups are popular with collectors too.

This 3-D Victorian Christmas card depicts a nativity scene, possibly the flight from Bethlehem to Egypt.

shown with toys and feasts, whereas the poor person would be glad of an orange.

'The attraction is in the design and the messages. First you get the desire to collect, and then to improve and enlarge. Going out to find them was something my wife and I always did together, and I've carried on with it since she died in 1985. It was always a lovely feeling finding something we really liked.

'Now, at Christmas, I give displays and talks about them. They take older people back to happy memories of Christmas times when they were very young.

'Some people might consider my hobby eccentric, but I feel I'm saving the cards for the future. It's better than if they were just lost.'

BOOKS

Books that date from before the 1820s are for the connoisseur. Collectors admire them, but they are rare and expensive. After the mechanisation of bookmaking, more were made, but sadly the covers of many leather Victorian books produced from the 1830s became dry and brittle. The introduction of colour printing in the 1850s was the start of a golden age for books. Engraving, lithography and oil-coloured prints brought them to life and these are the books that are usually sought after. More ornate covers were designed, using gold and silver paints.

A book about a popular subject, which is also well produced, will carry a premium. Some people are attracted only to the contents, and the printing techniques don't matter so much. Highway code collector Nina Morgan has devoted years to the improvement of road safety, so she has focused on a particular theme. Other collectors may focus on an author or illustrator, or may only collect books of a certain era.

Some old books are still very cheap, particularly those about obscure subjects by unknown authors. But the ones that are most in demand are valued for their aesthetic and design qualities. A few decades ago, there was a vogue for tearing the colour prints out of books, so any collector should check for this. First editions are particularly collectable and can fetch thousands of pounds at auction (*see Pricing Books on page 144*).

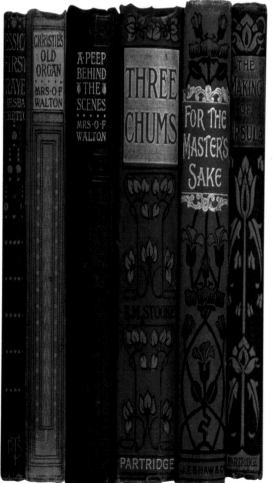

Before the advent of the paperback, all books had hard covers. They were usually beautifully decorated, especially on the spines. The dust jacket was often printed in eye-catching colours.

The books on the left were produced for children early in the twentieth century. Plain books sometimes had dust jackets, but it wasn't until the 1920s, when economic conditions made it impractical to decorate the covers, that dust jackets became common.

HIGHWAY CODES
Nina Morgan

'My son lives on in my collection', says Nina Morgan, MBE, a senior citizen from Exeter, who collects Highway Codes from all over the world.

'I'm not a magpie as such. I wouldn't collect thimbles or frogs, for example. I started collecting Highway Codes after my son, Chris, was killed in a road accident in 1969. I didn't want him to have died in vain.

'I collect them because I'm interested in road safety, and I work for road safety in Tanzania and Zambia as well as in the UK. I have some codes for countries that no longer exist, like Tanganyika (now Tanzania). There are always new ones coming out, like one for South Africa. Some are highly amusing; in Saudi Arabia drivers are instructed to give way to camels.

'My husband was a government pilot, and spent a lot of time in Africa so I've travelled a lot. The USA codes are very interesting. I read them through and think "we could do that in the UK to improve driving". Each State has its own code. Some States are 'dry' – you can't even transport alcohol in your car.

'I collect for the different designs, too. The Ethiopean one is a pretty little book with pull-out road signs. I've asked our ministers whether we could have a cover for the British Highway Code that would make people want to read it.

'I've had lots of letters from people who watched *Collectors' Lot*. One man sent me an army manual for drivers in Germany that he'd nurtured for fifty years.'

The first British Highway Code came out in 1932. Nina has a rare copy – a small brown book which cost 1d. She is the only collector in this field according to Road Safety Officers in the UK. For lots of variety, try the Australian codes.

British Highway Codes are not known for their attention-grabbing covers. This edition dates from the 1970s.

THE HIGHWAY CODE

HMSO 25p net

PRICING BOOKS

The general rule when predicting the price of a book is that the most aesthetically pleasing books – with illustrations by a talented artist, maybe from the early days of colour printing when the quality was high – will command the highest prices. It may be surprising to learn that not all old books appreciate in value. The family Bible, for instance, which would have cost a small fortune in Victorian times, is worth comparatively little today. For collectors, the interest in such a Bible may lie in the records of family history which were often written inside them. Conversely, books don't have to be very old to be valuable. Even good illustrators and writers from the 1970s are collectable now.

The price that you pay for a book or annual will depend on the rarity, popularity and condition and whether or not it is a first edition. Most recently published books won't cost more than £10 and in junk shops they're often selling for just a few pence. But once you start to refine your collection, and you're considering spending more, there's no substitute for knowledge and experience.

When buying a book or annual, there are a few things that you should look at. Firstly, examine the general condition of the book – it shouldn't have missing pages or be marked or worn. Secondly, if it is an early illustrated book, look to see whether the colour plates are intact and of good quality.

First editions of classics are worth more than later editions, but they can sometimes be hard to find. *Jane Eyre*, for example, has been reprinted just about every year since it was first published in 1847. Try looking inside the book, at the first few pages, but that isn't always reliable and you would have to know when the book was first published. First editions rarely surface at car boot sales these days.

The quality of the subject matter and the author's credibility also affect the price. Certain issues of the post-war *Eagle*, for example, used science fiction writer Arthur C. Clarke. The use of talented illustrators also makes a difference – *Little Folks* featured Kate Greenaway from 1879–90.

Books produced in the 1920s and 1930s had plain covers, but came in a decorative dust jacket, and few of these have survived. Most hard backs still come with a wrapper. In fact, this will usually enhance the book's value – a first edition of Ian Fleming's *Casino Royale* with a dust jacket would cost £3,000, without one, it could go for as little as £300. You are unlikely to find a copy with dust jacket – the reason they cost so much is that they are so rare.

CARING FOR BOOKS

• Cold or damp may encourage mould to grow. A temperature of 65°F (18°C) should be high enough to kill off the spores.

• Acid may migrate from the pages of early Victorian books. Only professional bleaching can remove the brown marks that will result.

CHILDREN'S PUBLICATIONS

There were very few books specially written for children, before the nineteenth century. *Gulliver's Travels*, by Jonathan Swift, springs to mind. It was first published in 1726, but was actually written as an adult book: a hard-hitting political satire, commenting on the goings on between the Whigs and the Tories. That's probably why *Alice's Adventures in Wonderland* was so popular when it was published in 1866. Among the first books that most people would have been able to afford were Chapbooks. These story books, with drawings, were tiny enough to be carried by the village peddler, or chapman as he was called, in the trays that he hung around his neck. They were about three inches wide. They are very rare today and, if in good condition, can now cost

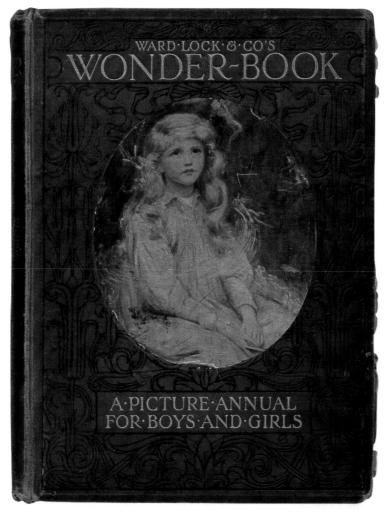

hundreds of pounds. Early pop-up books and first editions by well known authors and artists command good prices too. Look out for the earliest editions of classics, some of which have been reprinted many times. Most of the children's books that you'll come across will have been published since the 1950s and so won't be as expensive.

Annuals have been popular from the nineteenth century right up to the present day. If history is your interest, there's no better way to find out about the culture of a time than to look at the material published to influence the impressionable minds of young people. Not

Wonder-Book: A Picture Annual for Boys and Girls is an example of the books filled with heroic tales that were produced for children during the late nineteenth and early twentieth centuries.

surprisingly, perhaps, the annuals that became popular – including *Boys Own* and *Girls Own* (from 1879–1941) soft pedalled on blatant religious instruction. Instead, they got their message across by means of characters whose bravery and honesty won the day.

In the 1920s, the face of annuals changed forever when D.C. Thomson brought out 'the big five': *Rover*, *The Wizard*, *Skipper*, *Hotspur* and *Adventure Land*. While previous annuals had thrived on the public school image, perhaps reflecting their readers, this new breed was robust and brash, featuring scallywags caught up in wild adventures.

Probably the most successful author of children's books in the twentieth century is Enid Blyton. Her daughter, Gillian Baverstock, who is building a collection of her works, explains the secret of her mother's success: 'People recognise that through her stories she has helped more children to read over a period of seventy years than any other writer – and not only English-speaking children since the books are translated into more than forty languages. They tell me that they loved the books as children and learned a lot from them; they also loved the artists she chose to illustrate the books and so want to get the old hard back editions. I think that nostalgia has a great deal to do with the growing market for Blyton second hand books.

'Most of the books have been published in several editions and re-illustrated. Modern editions can look very different from those we loved as children. Noddy has just been re-drawn and for me has lost the attraction that the original artists gave him. Much of this artwork was sold at Sotheby's in October 1997 and the early work fetched enormous prices.'

The world of children's book collecting is as complex as you wish to make it. If you are happy to make an attractive, interesting collection from a historical or literary point of view, there are many bargains amongst later impressions of classics. If you are hoping for the collection to appreciate in value one day, you will need to be more careful in what you buy, and you will probably have to spend more money. To collect in this way it is advisable to consult a specialist magazine, such as *Book and Magazine Collector*.

In the end, any collector decides for him- or herself what is 'valuable'. Experienced collectors learned by steeping themselves in a subject. Everyone knows, at one level or another, why a particular book – or any other collectable for that matter – is simply too tempting to be left on the shelf.

Collector's Tip

'*When buying or selling at auction check how much commission will be due.*'

ENID BLYTON
Gillian Baverstock

'Although I knew that my mother had many letters from children, I wasn't really aware of her being famous until I was fourteen, when I met other young people who had read her books and enjoyed them just as I had,' says Gillian Baverstock, now half-way to completing her collection of her mother's books and related ephemera.

'By the time I was born, she had done much educational writing and had published several collections of short stories. When I was five and just starting to read, she wrote her first long book, called *The Adventures of the Wishing Chair*. As I matured, she published books for older children, such as *The Famous Five* when I was nearly ten and *The Island of Adventure* when I was twelve.

'I lost the access to Enid Blyton's library of file copies when the copyrights were sold two years ago. I still had a number of books from my childhood and with these as the nucleus I began forming my own collection. I am becoming fussier now, trying to find good first editions in dust wrappers. Fortunately, I knew which were the best book collectors to contact as I had completed a collection of Noddy books for the copyright holding company earlier.

'Books can be picked up in car boot or jumble sales for a few pence and it is still possible to find a first edition in this way. For better quality and rare books, visit second-hand bookshops or go to private collectors. Most books with dust wrappers can be bought for under £10. On the other hand, a hard-to-find first edition in good condition might cost more than £100.'

Photograph of Gillian in her garden. Beside her, in his red and yellow taxi, is a model of one of her mother's most enduring characters, Noddy. The car was made to promote the 1990s television series.

Collectors' Lot *Presenters*

Jethro Marles

Jethro Marles, who lives in Devon, has been involved with *Collectors' Lot* since the series began. His collecting interest and business activities concentrate on fine jewellery.

'Collecting becomes a way of life. When I was new to the business twenty years ago, there was a "hunting" aspect to it all. I'd buy an object that appealed and study it closely, learning a bit more through having the piece. As knowledge develops with experience, your tastes change and the items you used to think were special often lose their appeal. When I worked as an auctioneer, I was the custodian of sale items for several months at a time. In a way I possessed them, even though I didn't own them. Seeing so many fine pieces made it difficult to decide to collect any one thing.

'When you're my age with a family and a mortgage, you put money into necessities. We have a few pieces of antique furniture that we like, but I'm happy to mix the new with the old. With boisterous children, playful cats and limited funds, now isn't the time to collect Martinware pottery birds, which I love. However, I do have the beginnings of a collection of animal sculptures, including a sly fox and a wise owl by Jenny Hale.'

Jethro's Tips

'If you're collecting with a view to making a valuable investment, objects sold specifically to appeal to collectors are risky. You are generally safer with quality, rarity, beauty and items with a track record. Before spending a substantial sum, or parting with a collection or item you don't know the value of, do get the opinion of at least one expert, preferably two or more. Auction houses, collectors' societies and clubs, magazines and price guides are good sources of information.'

Robert Opie

Robert Opie has featured on *Collectors' Lot* since the outset. At first he organised the competition, more recently he has presented items and interviewed collectors.

'I grew up in a collecting environment. My father had built an outstanding collection of children's books and, in a sense, I was able to do my "apprenticeship" under his guidance. I collected the usual things – stamps, coins and Matchbox toys – but all the time I was looking for a subject that had not been explored.

'When I was sixteen I found an area that was not being saved and recorded – packaging and promotion material. I was enjoying some chocolate Munchies at the time and thought, "If I throw away this packet, a piece of our social history will be lost." From that moment I saved everything; later I started to study the extraordinary story of our consumer society.

'I still remember the excitement of looking for early packaging in Portobello Road when no-one else had done it before. Five years later, in 1975, I put together an exhibition at the Victoria & Albert Museum, the first of its kind, which led to my opening the Museum of Advertising and Packaging at Gloucester.

'My philosophy has been to fit the things I collect into the overall culture of society, so I needed to understand how and why things have happened. My approach to collecting is much more like that of a social historian; and it's good to share my interests through the books I have written.'

Robert's Tips

'Think about what you're trying to achieve and what you want your collection to do. This is an ongoing process. By keeping to your purpose, you are less likely to accumulate things for no reason – but whatever else, have fun.'

Laura Beaumont

Laura Beaumont shares her London home with Bill Oddie, their twelve-year-old daughter and enough Mickey Mouse paraphernalia to 'hurt your eyes'. Besides being a *Collectors' Lot* presenter she's become a guru of humourous consumables.

'I think if you probe deeply enough everybody collects something, but there's a fine line between hoarder and collector.'

'I'm attracted to the jolly cheery playfulness of it all, so it doesn't matter what age it is. The old expensive stuff is not what it's about for me. The accumulative effect looks spectacular. Disney is just the tip of the iceberg. Look in any of my rooms and they're so cluttered a lot of people would scream. I just like things around. Relatives have died and I've ended up with things I can't part with.

'Sometimes, I get fed up with the primary colours. There are times when I want a flame thrower to come in and torch it, then I could paint the whole lot white – but the feeling passes. I think our daughter is secretly proud of it, although she feigns embarrassment. There's a jungle bedroom and a seaside land-ing, so she's grown up with plastic lobsters.

'I don't dust them. I'm of the Quentin Crisp school of thought – after the first five years dust doesn't get any worse.'

Laura's Tips
'If everyone knows you collect something, then people just start giving you things. So tell people. You can let one collection lead to another – just shift your focus.' At Disney World (Laura's family has been seven times) there is an area devoted to 1950s comedy, and from this she became interested in Lucille Ball. After that dolls, books and fridge magnets, to do with the actress turned up.

Lorne Spicer

Lorne Spicer's early collecting habits now earn her a living as a writer and presenter and as co-editor of *Collect It* magazine.

'As a small child I'd go to fairs with my mum. One of the first things I was allowed to do on my own was to go into town. I used to go to jumble sales and come home with bin liners full of stuff. I soon learnt that if I was sweet and polite people would let me have something for virtually nothing. Later I started collecting leather books, which were cheap and affordable. I remember being thrilled when I bought a first edition that turned out to be worth £80.

'I love weird and whacky things. Recently I bought a 1930s doll's mangle set, which looks quite cute in the kitchen. I collect kitchenalia and Royal Winton moulded relief ware at present. I love the activity of collecting. Money is secondary, but I always buy new limited editions by Royal Doulton because they have a habit of immediately going up in value. Often, once a collection is nearly complete, I find the challenge is gone and I'm ready to start again. I've always got a couple of collections on the go.'

Lorne's Tips
'Do be sure that you know when you're buying a reproduction. Dealers should know and inform you, but sometimes they don't! The golden rule is "buyer beware". Equally, don't assume there are no bargains left to be found. I recently found a rare Wade golliwog at the Newark Antiques Fair and the only known example of a Royal Winton flowerseller figure. But you only pick up bargains after learning all you can about collecting and making a few mistakes along the way!'

Finding Out More

Organisations for Collectors

The following trade organisations represent their members, who are antiques dealers (at the more expensive end of the market) and give information and advice to consumers. They administer codes of practice that protect consumers in dispute with their members.

British Antique Dealers' Association (BADA), 20 Rutland Gate, London SW7 1BD. Tel: 0171 589 4128. Fax: 0171 581 9083. Has 400 members – top dealers in the country. List of members and addresses and areas in which they specialise on application. They will also provide BADA customs clearance certificates and advice if you are sending goods abroad.

LAPADA The Association of Art and Antique Dealers, 535 King's Rd, London SW10 OSZ. Tel: 0171 823 3511. Fax: 0171 823 3522. e-mail:lapada@lapada.co.uk.
Website: http://www.lapada.co.uk/lapada/
LAPADA has over 700 members. Free computerised information for buyers or sellers. Free directory of members on application.

Guides with Diary Listings

Antiques Bulletin. Tel: 0121 681 8002. Biannual magazine.

Antique Collecting, the magazine of the Antique Collectors' Club. Published ten times a year (subscription only), includes regional and specialist clubs.

Antique Dealer and Collectors' Guide, a monthly magazine that lists monthly fairs. Available from newsagents. Tel: 0181 861 0690. e-mail: antiquedealercollectorsguide@ukbusiness.com Website: http://www.ukbusiness.com/antiquedealercollectorsguide

Antiques Diary Guide to regional antique and collectors' fairs, published bi-monthly. Tel: 0118 940 2165.

Antiques Fairs Guide. Tel: 0121 681 8002. Biannual guide.

Collect It. Tel: 01344 868280. Monthly magazine for collectors.

Collectors' Gazette. Specialist newspaper for toy collectors. Mostly die-casts, but some games. Monthly from newsagents.

Collectors Guide, The International Magazine for Dealers and Collectors. Subscriptions Tel: 0181 861 0690. Monthly £2.75.

Book Publishers for Collectors

Old catalogues, published by each of the main auction houses are often available for sale after an auction – with the prices that items sold for listed on a separate paper. These are part illustrated and give a good idea of price and quality.

Antique Collectors' Club (ACC), 5 Church Street, Woodbridge, Suffolk IP12 1DS. Tel: 01394 385501 Fax: 01394 384434. Publishes a wide range of reference books on fine arts and antiques. Free catalogue available on request.

Christie's Books, 1 Langley Lane, London SW8 1TH. Tel: 0171 389 2242. Collectors' Book Choice is a catalogue of books that are of interest to collectors.

Francis Joseph Publications, 15 St Swithuns Road, London SE13 6RW. Tel: 0181 318 9580. Publishes informative and well illustrated guides, with prices, on a wide range of twentieth-century ceramics and glass, including Susie Cooper, Clarice Cliff, Carlton Ware, Moorcroft and Art Deco.

Millers Reed Book Services Ltd, PO Box 5, Rushden, Northants NN10 6YX. Produces many useful guides and also runs a club. Write for details.

Richard Dennis Publications, The Old Chapel, Shepton Beauchamp, Ilminster, Somerset, TA19 OLE. Tel: 01460 242009. Has a selection of books for collectors.

Schiffer Books, distributed in the UK by Bushwood Books, 84 Bushwood Rd, Kew Gardens, Surrey TW9 3BQ. Tel: 0181 948 8119. Fax: 0181 948 3232. Publishes books on a huge array of collectables as well as on antiques and design.

Shire Publications, Cromwell House, Church Street, Princes Risborough, Bucks HP27 9AA. Tel: 01844 344301. Fax: 01844 347080. Known for modestly priced books written by enthusiasts and experts on over 600 topics, of interest to both new and established collectors.

Sotheby's Bookshop, 34–5 New Bond Street, London W1Y 8YX. Tel: 0171 493 8080. Fax: 0171 408 5909. Also publishes a mail order catalogue of books on all aspects of antiques.

General Books for Collectors

Guide to the Antique Shops of Britain (Antique Collectors' Club Ltd). The 1998/9 edition of this invaluable guide is now out.

Jackson's Silver and Gold Marks of England, Scotland & Ireland edited by Ian Pickford (Antique Collectors Club, £49.95). The 'bible' for silver collectors.

The Lyle Price Guides cover several subjects, including printed collectables, also dolls and toys, clocks and watches, Art Nouveau and Art Deco. Cost around £15, even out of date ones can give a good idea of relative prices, but shouldn't be relied on too heavily, the markets fluctuate.

Miller's Understanding Antiques by Judith and Martin Miller, General Editors (Paperback £14.99).

Museums and Galleries in Great Britain and Ireland. A detailed guide to museums and art galleries open to the general public. (Hobsons Publishing, £8.95 from bookshops or through Bibliof Tel: 01403 710851.)

Pocket Edition Jackson's Hallmarks of England, Scotland & Ireland by Ian Pickford (Antique Collectors Club £6.95 paperback).

Auction Houses

There are four main auction houses; all have branches or representatives nationwide. They are usually happy to give valuations on objects you are considering selling. For other local auction houses, freephone: Talking Pages 0800 600 900.

Bonhams, Montpelier St, London SW7 Tel: 0171 393 3900. http://www.bonhams.com/

Christie's, 8 King Street, St. James's London SW1Y 6QT. Tel: 0171 839 9060. Website: http://www.christies.com
Christie's South Kensington (where you're likely to find 'collectables' and 'decorative arts' as well as antiques), 85 Old Brompton Road, London SW7 3LD. Tel: 0171 581 7611.

Phillips, Blenstock House, 101 New Bond St, London W1. Tel: 0171 629 6602. Website: http://www.phillips-auctions.com

Sotheby's, 34–5 New Bond St, London W1. Tel: 0171 493 8080. Website: http://www.sothebys.com

Other Useful Organisations

English Tourist Board, Thames Tower, Black's Rd, Hammersmith, London W6 9EL. Tel: 0181 846 9000.

The National Trust, PO Box 39, Bromley, Kent BR1 3XL. Tel: 0181 315 1111. Website: www.ukindex.co.uk/nationaltrust/

The National Trust for Scotland, 5 Charlotte Square, Edinburgh EH2 4DU. Tel: 0131 226 5922. Fax: 0131 243 9302.

For other tourist centres, freephone Talking Pages: 0800 600 900.

Internet Sites of Interest to Collectors

The *Collectors' Lot* website is available via the Channel 4 website at http://www.channel4.com (click on 'Back-up' in the main menu).

http://www.albany.edu/~ss4569/autograph.html
Information for autograph hunters.

http://www/gwdg.de/~ifbg/collect.html
An index of sites for general information on collecting and specific collectables.

http://www.psychol.ulc.ac.uk/jonathan.farringdon/buxton.html
UK antiques information page.

http://ww.yahoo.co.uk/Recreation/Hobbies_andCrafts_/Collecting
A comprehensive listing of sites for collectors of all persuasions from stamps to action figures to typewriters.

Restoration and Repair

ABPR (Association of British Picture Restorers), Station Avenue, Kew, Surrey TW9 3QA. Tel: 0181 948 5644.

British Antique Furniture Restorers' Association (BAFRA), The Old Rectory, Warmwell, Dorchester, Dorset DT2 8HQ. Tel: 01305 854822. Fax: 01305 852104. They can point you towards a local restorer by phone, or you can invest £6.25 (inc p & p) in their BAFRA Guide. This sixty-page book names all members and includes articles by furniture experts.

National Association of Goldsmiths, 78 Luke Street, London EC2A 4PY. Tel: 0171 613 4445. Can provide names of jewellers in your area who may advise on quality and repair.

Chapter One ~ A Touch of Class

COLLECTORS' CLUBS, SOCIETIES AND MUSEUMS
Bramah Museum of Tea and Coffee, Clove Building, McGuire Street, London. SE1 2NQ. Tel: 0171 378 0222. Large display of tea and coffee pots. The story of the tea and coffee trades.

Broadfield House Glass Museum, Compton Drive, Kingswinford, West Midlands, DY6 9NS. Tel: 01384 812745. Internationally recognised centre for the study and enjoyment of glass-making. Besides the collections, attractions include a working glass studio, archive and library (by appointment). Tells the story of British glass, concentrating on the nineteenth century, which is known as The Golden Age of Stourbridge Glass.

Cambridge Paperweight Circle, 34 Huxley Road, Welling, Kent, UK. Tel: 0181 303 4663. Write to the chairman, enclosing a sae for details. Holds three meetings a year, with guest speakers, issues a newsletter and organises visits to factories.

Clarice Cliff Collector's Club, Leonard Griffin, Fantasque House, Tennis Drive, The Park, Nottingham NG7 1AE. Send sae for membership details.

Crafts Council, 44a Pentonville Road, London N1 9BY. Tel: 0171 278 7700. Website: http://www.craftscouncil.org.uk e-mail: info@craftscouncil.org.uk. Exhibitions held and also arranges touring exhibitions. Its publication *Crafts Magazine* gives comprehensive listings and features on crafts in the UK.

Egg-cup Collectors' Club of Great Britain (ECCC). Tel: 01202 944009. Run by Audrey Diamond. Subscription of £6 gives your four newletters with articles and details of swaps and meetings.

FACTORY VISITS
Caithness Glass, Inveralmond, Perth PH1 3TZ. Tel: 01738 637 373. Visitors' Centre is open seven days, but glass-making happens Monday–Friday 9am–4.30pm.

Gladstone Working Pottery Museum, Stoke-on-Trent ST3 1PQ. Tel: 01782 319232. Experience life in an Edwardian pottery. Demonstrations and workshops can be arranged.

Perthshire Paperweights, Crieff. Tel: 01764 654014. Monday–Thursday 9am–4pm, Friday 9am–2pm.

Selkirk Glass, Dunsdale Haugh, Selkirk, TD7 5EF. Tel 01750 20954. Monday–Friday 9am–4.30pm, Saturday 11am–3pm.

SPECIALIST GALLERIES AND SERVICES
Dr Steele's Stop Smoking Clinic, University Hospital of South Manchester, Withington M20. Tel: 0161 445 3423. One of Britain's few free NHS smoking cessation clinics.

The London Glass Fair is held every few months, dates from P&A. Tel: 0181 543 5075

Pullman Gallery Ltd, 14 King Street, St James's, London SW1Y 6QU. Tel: 0171 930 9595. Simon Khachadourian's cocktail shakers are on display at his new shop. Pullman also has a wide selection of *objets de luxe* dating from 1880 to around 1950, including smoking accessories, posters, Lalique collectables and luggage.

The Stone Gallery, 93 High St, Burford, Oxfordshire.
Tel: 01993 823302. Veral Marshall's gallery, the largest classical collection of paperweights on display and for sale.

Andy Thornton Architectural Antiques Ltd, Victoria Mills, Stainland Rd, Greetland, Halifax, W. Yorks. HX4 8AD.
Tel: 01422 377 314. Four-storey ex-mill building crammed to the eaves with all sorts from bathroom fittings to Coca-Cola machines from the 1950s to a complete pharmacy interior.

PUBLICATIONS
Art Deco Ceramics by Jane Hay (Little, Brown and Company, £8.99). A clearly written and well illustrated guide for the beginner. Other titles in this series are: *Small Silver Tableware* by Stephen Helliwell; *Teapots, The Connoisseur's Guide* by Paul Tippett and *Art Nouveau Jewellery* by David Lancaster.

Ceramics of the 1950s by Graham McLaren (Shire Publications £3.95).

Coalport 1795–1926 by Michael Messenger (Antique Collectors' Club).

http://www.lattimore.co.uk/deco/
Online publication dealing with Art Deco in Britain, lists fairs, dealers and collectors' clubs.

Novelty Teapots: 350 Years of Art and Design by Edward Bramah (available from the Bramah Museum, see address above, £38).

Paperweights by Pat Reilly, (Apple Press, Quintet, £8.99)

Treasures in your Home, editor Michael Wright (Readers Digest).

Chapter Two ~ Glitter and Gladrags

COLLECTORS' CLUBS, SOCIETIES AND MUSEUMS
The Bead Society, 1 Casburn Lane, Burwell, Cambridgeshire. CB5 OED. Send sae for membership form.

British Compact Collectors' Society, PO Box 131, Woking, Surrey GU24 9YR. Send sae for details. Organise regional meetings, newsletters and conventions.

The Button Museum, 13 Kyrle Street, Ross-on-Wye, Herefordshire HR9 7DB. Tel: 01989 566089.

The Costume Society, 56 Wareham Rd, Lytchett Matravers, Poole, Dorset BH16 6DS.
Send sae for details.

The Fan Museum, 12 Crooms Hill, Greenwich, London SE10 8ER. Tel: 0181 305 1441.

Forge Mill Needle Museum, Redditch. Tel: 01527 62509.
Celebrates the history of needle making and sewing accessories.

Gallery of English Costume, Platt Hall, Rusholme, Manchester M14 5LL. Tel: 0161 224 5217.

Hat Works, Unit 42, Offerton Industrial Estate, Hempshaw Lane, Offerton, Stockport. Tel: 0161 474 4460.
A museum of hats and of the Stockport hatting industry.

Web site: www.stockportmbc.gov.uk/heritage/

Hope House Costume Museum and Restoration Workshop, Derbyshire. Tel: 01335 310318 or 01335 370915. Houses Notty Hornblower's collection of costumes from 1840 to the 1970s. Visits by appointment only.

Museum of Childhood, Sudbury Hall Pickford's House, 41 Friar Gate, Derby. Tel: 0132 255363. For children's costumes and toys.

Museum of Costume, The Assembly Rooms, Bennett Street, Bath, BA1 2QH. Tel: 01225 477789.

The Silk Museum, Heritage Centre, Roe St, Macclesfield, Cheshire Tel: 01625 613210. Story of the silk industry.

National Association of Goldsmiths, 78a Luke Street, London EC2A 4PY. Tel: 0171 613 4445. Can name some valuers and jewellers in your area who may advise on quality and repair.

Society of Jewellery Historians, c/o Kenneth Snowman, 14 Ryefold Road, Wimbledon Park, SW19, 8BZ.

UK Perfume Bottle Collectors' Club, Linda Brine, PO Box 1936, Bath BA1 3SD.

SPECIALIST SHOPS AND SERVICES
Almeh Amira (aka Christine Hall). Tel: 01580 850687.
Performs and teaches oriental dance. She entertains at festivals, restaurants and wedding receptions (no 'men-only' events) and organises workshops.

Antique Clothing Store, 282 Portobello Road, London W10 5TE. Where some of today's top designers shop for inspiration.

Echoes, Pat and Richard Oldman, Halifax Road, Todmorden, Yorks. Tel: 01706 817505.
An important resource for designers or historians, as well as an Aladdin's cave for anyone interested in buying old clothes or textiles.

Sparkle Moore, The Girl Can't Help It, Alfie's Antiques Market, 13–25 Church Street, Marylebone, London NW8.
Tel: 0171 723 0564. Twentieth-century pin-up and period clothing accessories and collectables.

PUBLICATIONS
The Collectors Guide to Fans by Susan Mayor (Studio Editions, 1995, £4.99).

The Hat, Trends and Traditions by Madeleine Ginsburg (Studio Editions, 1990).

Jewellery 1789–1910 by Shirley Bury (Antique Collectors' Club, £75 for a two-volume set, £39 for a single volume).

Old Jewellery by Duncan James (Shire Publications £4.95). Explains manufacturing techniques and dating clues.

Sentimental Jewellery by Ann Louise Luthi (Shire Publications, £3.95).

The Subversive Stitch, Embroidery and the Making of the Feminine by Rozsika Parker (The Women's Press).

*Understanding Jew*ellery by D. Bennett and D. Mascetti (Antique Collectors' Club). Practical guide with values for the collector.

Chapter Three ~ Stargazing

COLLECTORS' CLUBS, SOCIETIES AND MUSEUMS
British Film Institute. Tel: 0171 255 1444

The British Music Hall Society, c/o Brodie & Middleton, 68 Drury Lane, London WC2B 5SP. Send a sae for a list of societies.

Dad's Army Society, J. A. Wheeler, Commander-in-Chief, 8 Sinodun Rd, Wallingford, Oxon, OX10 8AA. Write for information.

Nick Bennett, 20c Bradshawgate, Leigh, Lancashire WN7 4LX. Website: http://www.lasercc.demon.co.uk/bond.htm Post-war collectable toys by mail order.

The Ivor Novello Society, Nick Gaze & Chris Fansom, 188 Church Drive, Quedgeley, Gloucestershire GL2 4US. Tel: 01452 720182. Website: http://www.geocities.com/Broadway/Balcony/2703/ e-mail: NoveloScot@aol.com

The James Bond 007 International Fan Club and Archive, PO Box 007, Addlestone, Surrey KT15 1DY.

Marilyn Lives Society, Michelle Morgan's website: http://www.doheny.demon.co.uk

National Film Theatre, South Bank, Waterloo, London SE1 8XT. Tel: 0171 928 3535. Where you can catch up on all the golden oldies missed first time around. You can also visit the NFT's interactive Museum of the Moving Image.

The Theatre Museum, 1E Tavistock Street, London WC2E 7PA. Tel: 0171 836 7891. Has a huge collection of theatre playbills, programmes, prompt books, manuscripts, autographed letters and reviews covering thousands of productions.

SPECIALIST SHOPS AND SERVICES
Cinema Book Shop, Great Russell Street, London. Enclose sae for enquiries.

Collectors Record Centre, York Street, Twickenham. Tel: 0181 891 5550. Shirley Abrey finds many of her 1960s albums here.

Flashbacks, 6 Silver Place, London W1. Tel: 0171 437 8562. Film memorabilia specialists.

Memoryville, 228 Ellan Hay Rd, Bradley Stoke South, Bristol BS12 OHF. Tel: 01179 854690. Kelvin Forde arranges Rock 'n' Roll weekends at venues in the UK and on the Mediterranean.

Purple Haze, 38 Eastlake Walk, Drake Circus, Plymouth PL1 1BX. Tel: 01752 254136. Sci-fi, comic and cult TV memorabilia

Radio Days, 87 Lower Marsh, London SE1. Tel: 0171 928 0800.

Vintage Magazine Shop, 39–43 Brewer Street, London W1R 3FD. Tel: 0171 439 8525. Specialises in film, fashion and music magazines.

PUBLICATIONS
Marilyn's Addresses by Michelle Finn, (Smith Gryphon, London N1 9UU, 1995, £9.99).

Miller's Rock and Pop Memorabilia by Stephen Maycock (Reed International Books, £14.99).

Phillips Collector's Guide to Rock and Pop by Alison Fox (£6.95). Price guide and handy list of fan club addresses.

The Star Wars Archives by M. Cotta Vaz et al (Virgin Books, £23). Props, costumes, models and artwork from the films.

Chapter Four ~ Pleasure and Play

COLLECTORS' CLUBS, SOCIETIES AND MUSEUMS
Association of Football Badge Collectors, 18 Hinton Street, Fairfield, Liverpool L6 3AR. Tel: 0151 260 0554. Send sae for details.

The Bear Museum, 38 Dragon St, Petersfield GU31 4JJ. Tel: 01730 265108.

Bethnal Green Museum of Childhood, Cambridge Heath Road, London E2 9PA. Tel: 0181 981 1711. Large collection of every kind of toy and game.

British Marble Board of Control, c/o 50 Ham Road, Worthing Sussex, NN11 2QX. For collectors and players, organises annual championship.

British Model Soldiers' Society, Mark Gilbert (Secretary), 50 Putney Road, Enfield, Middx EN3 6NN. Tel: 01992 715 621. Monthly meetings and branches nationwide.

Cricket Memorabilia Society, 29 Highclere Road, Higher Crumpsall, Manchester M8 4WH. Tel: 0161 740 3714. Send sae for details.

Doll Club of Great Britain, c/o Faith Eaton, sae to 16 Clifton Gardens, London W9 1DT. Collectors of antique dolls.

The English Playing Card Society, 11 Pierrepoint Street, Bath BA1 1LA. Tel: 01225 465218. Publish a newsletter.

The Forbidden Corner, The Tupgill Park Estate, Coverham, Middleham, Leyburn, North Yorkshire. Johnny and Wendy Reeves. Tel: 01969 640638.
Malcolm Tempest designed this fantasy garden, which is open to the public between April and October. Ring for opening times.

Gnome Reserve, West Putford, Nr Bradworthy, North Devon. Tel: 01409 241 435. Open daily from 21 March until end of October, 10am–6pm. Adults: £1.75, children 3–16: £1.25, under 3: free, OAPs: £1.50.

The Hornby Railway Collectors, Association, 1 Park Street, Stapleford, Nottingham, NG9 8EU. Tel: 0115 949 7194. Exists to preserve and play with Hornby trains. Worldwide organisation which produces a monthly magazine which tells all about the people involved with Hornby trains.

The House on the Hill Toy Museum, Nr Mountfitchit Castle, Stansted, Essex CM24 8SP. Tel: 01279 813237. One of the largest toy museums in the country.

Lamport Hall, Northamptonshire NN6 9HD. Tel: 01604 686272. Open Sundays and Bank Holiday Mondays (also Thursdays in July and August) from Easter until end of September, 2.15–5.15pm. Admission £1.50.

Museum of Childhood, 42 High Street, Edinburgh EH1 1TG. Tel: 0131 225 2424. Five public galleries hold displays of indoor and outdoor games.

Pinball Owners' Association, PO Box 122, Cambridge CB1 4AH. Send sae for details. Has a monthly magazine and arranges conventions with a 100 machines set up.

Pollock's Toy Museum, 1 Scala Street, London W1P 1LT. Tel: 0171 636 3452. Model theatres, antique board and card games.

Stranger's Hall Museum of Domestic Life, Charing Cross, Norwich NR2 4AL. Tel: 01603 667229. A very good collection of toys and games which can be made available to researchers by appointment only.

SPECIALIST SHOPS AND SERVICES
David Bridgewater, Heather Cottage, Lansdown, Bath BA1 9BL. Tel: 01225 463435. Vintage garden tools and garden sculptures. View by appointment only.

Dave Cooper, Clarendon, Parsonage Road, Herne Bay, Kent, CT6 5TA. Tel: 01227 742222. Wooden jigsaw puzzles cut to order.

Crowther of Syon Lodge, Busch Corner, London Road, Isleworth, Middlesex TW7 5B11.
Website: http//www.crowther-syon-lodge.co.uk
Vintage garden ornaments.

Barrie E Ellen, 262 London Road, Westcliff-on-Sea, Essex. Tel: 01702 338763. Second-hand bookseller who specialises in chess books.

Marksman. Tel: 0181 992 0132. A mail-order business run by collector and maker Michael Ellis, sells reasonably priced 'starter packs' of fifty plastic soldiers.

Rink Bowls Equipment, 7 Eastfield Road, Lent Rise, Burnham, Slough SL1 7EH. Tel: 01628 668300. Mary Price's shop.

R. Somerville Playing Cards, 82 Canongate, the Royal Mile, Edinburgh, EH8 8BZ, Scotland. Tel: 0131 556 5225. Sells antique and modern playing cards and tarot.

PUBLICATIONS
British Jigsaw Puzzles of the Twentieth Century by Tom Tyler (Richard Dennis Publications).

Collectors' Gazette. Monthly newspaper for toy collectors, mostly covers die-casts, but some games.

A Collector's Guide to Games and Puzzles by Caroline Goodfellow (Apple Press, £9.95).

Dolls by Olivia Bristol (De Agostini, 1997). The antique doll expert at Christie's South Kensington.

http//www.salvo.co.uk
Information about reclaimed materials for gardens, includes pages about craftspeople and dealers.

The Plastic Warrior Magazine. Contact Brian Garrick for details. Tel: 0181 744 2014. Organises conventions for plastic figure collectors.

The Ultimate Doll Book by Caroline Goodfellow (Dorling Kindersley, 1993, £15.99).

Chapter Five ~ The Way We Were

COLLECTORS' CLUBS, SOCIETIES AND MUSEUMS
Abbey House Museum, Abbey Rd, Kirkstall, Leeds LS5 3EH. Tel: 0113 275 5821. Tells a picturesque tale of Victorian social history, including a shop window full of Burmantofts domestic pottery.

The Commemorative Collectors' Society, Secretary Steven Jackson, Lumless House, Gainsborough Rd, Winthorpe, Newark, Notts NG24 2NR.

D-Day Invasion Museum, Museum Road, Southsea, Portsmouth. Tel: 01705 827261.

National Monuments Records Centre, Kemble Drive, Swindon, SN2 2GZ. Tel: 01793 414 600. England's architectural and archaeological archive, also holds over four million aerial photographs. Large search room with free open access. Remote enquiry service. London records held at 55 Blandford Street London, W1H 3AF. Tel: 0171 208 8200.

The Pump House: The People's Museum, Left Bank, Bridge Street, Manchester M3 3ER. Tel: 0161 839 6061.
Has an important collection of union banners.

Rejectamenta (the Nostalgia Centre), Earnley Gardens, 133 Almodington Lane, Earnely, Chichester, West Sussex PO20 7JR. Tel: 01243 868725. Stella Mitchell's museum of twentieth-century social history.

Royal Armouries Museum of Artillery, Fort Nelson, Down End Road, Portsdown Hill, Fareham, PO17 6AN. Tel: 01329 233734 Artillery from pre-gunpowder days up to the present.

Tangmere Military Aviation Museum, Tangmere Airfield, Tangmere, Chichester, West Sussex, PO20 6ES. Tel: 01243 775223. Open 10am–5pm.

Thomas Cook Archives. Tel: 0171 408 4175.
Strictly by appointment, Monday to Friday 10am–4pm. Research facility only.

Wigan Pier, Wallgate, Wigan Tel: 01942 244888.
On the Leeds and Liverpool canal, Wigan Pier used to be used for transport at the heart of the coalmining and textile industries. It was the main means of transport for 'King Cotton' and 'King Coal'. Now it's a Heritage Centre with museum and working mill.

SPECIALIST SHOPS AND SERVICES

Cobwebs, 78 Northan Rd, Southampton, SO14 0PB. Tel: 01703 227458. Deals in collectables to do with the sea, and especially anything to do with oceanliners, including the *Titanic*.

The Goss and Crested China Club, 62 Murray Road, Horndean, Waterlooville, Hants PO8 9JL. Tel: 011705 597440. Trades in Goss and other souvenir ware

Kensal Green Cemetery, Harrow Road, London W12. The Friends of Kensal Green Cemetery organise guided tours every Sunday starting at 2pm (£4). Meet at the Anglican chapel in the centre of the cemetery. Visit to the catacombs on first Sunday of every month.

Royal Bed-and-Breakfast. Margaret Tyler, Heritage House, 77 The Fairway, North Wembley, Middlesex HA0 3TH. Tel: 0181 904 2452.

PUBLICATIONS:

The English Way of Death by Julian Litten (Robert Hale). This book is out of print, but almost every library had one so it should be reasonably easy to find.

Goss and other Crested China by Nicholas J. Pine (Shire Publications, 1994, £2.25).

Royal Commemoratives by Lincoln Hallinan (Shire Publications, 1997, £3.95).

Chapter Six ~ Time and Technology

COLLECTORS' CLUBS, SOCIETIES AND MUSEUMS

Amberley Museum, Amberley, Nr Arundel, West Sussex, BN18 9LT Tel: 01798 831 370. Fax: 01798 831831. http://www.fastnet.co.uk/amberley.museum/ Exhibits include radios, electrical appliances, bicycles, printing and bus memorabilia.

Ashorne Hall Nickelodeon, Ashorne Hall, Near Warwick CV33 9QN. Tel: 01926 651 444. Open Sundays and some days during the week from March to October, 1.30–5.30pm. The Hall houses Graham Whitehead's collection of mechanical musical instruments and there is a miniature railway in the garden. Graham also restores nickelodeons.

The British Watch and Clock Collectors Association, c/o Tony Woolven, 5 Cathedral Lane, Truro, Cornwall TR1 2QS. Tel: 01872 264010. Fax 01872 241953. E-mail: tony_Woolven@compuserve.com

The Cuckoo Clock Museum, The Tabley Old School Agency and Depot Chester Road, Tabley, Cheshire WA16 0HL Tel: 01565 633 039. Fax: 01565 750462.

Dold Exquisite Ltd Black Forest Clock Factory, The Tabley Old School Agency and Depot, Chester Road, Tabley, Cheshire WA16 0HL. Tel: 01565 633039. Fax: 01565 750462. Supplies Cuckoo Clocks to the trade.

Great Western Railway Museum, Farringdon Road, Swindon, Wilts. Tel: 01793 466555.

Historic Lighting Club of Great Britain, Correspondence Secretary, 23 Northcourt Road, Abingdon, Oxon OX14 1PW. For those interested in all forms of lighting from fires to gaslight.

The Lawnmower Museum at Trerice House, Kestle Mill, Nr Newquay, Cornwall TR8 4PG. Tel: 01637 875404.

Manor House Museum, Honey Hill, Bury St. Edmunds, Suffolk IP33 1HF. Tel: 01284 757076. Has a large collection of clocks and watches (as well as costume).

Museum of the History of Science, Old Ashmolean Building, Broad Street, Oxford OX1 3AZ. Tel: 01865 277280.

Musical Box Society of Great Britain, PO Box 299, Waterbeach, Cambridge, CB4 4PJ. Publishes a quarterly journal. Send sae for details.

National Museum of Photography, Film & Television, Pictureville, Bradford BD1 1NQ. Tel: 01274 727488.

The Old Lawnmowers Club, c/o Milton Keynes Museum, Southern Way, Wolverton, Milton Keynes MK12 5LT.

The Old Operating Theatre, Museum and Herb Garret, 9A St Thomas Street, London SE1 9RY. Tel: 0171 955 4791 or 0181 806 4325. Medical collectables.

Opthalmic Antiques Collectors Club, Stephen James, 4 The Cherry Orchard, Hadlow, Tonbridge, Kent TN11 0HU.

Photographic Collectors' Club of Great Britain, 5 Station Industrial Estate, Low Prudhoe, Northumbria, NE42, 6NP. Provides information, a newsletter six times a year and a glossy magazine.

Southern Electric Museum. Tel: 01202 480467. Open weekdays Easter to September, noon–4pm.

Sunrise Press, Spice House, 13, Belmont Road, Exeter, EX1 2HF. Tel: 01392 411565. Contact Jonathan Hill at the above address for information on the Vintage Communications Fair, held twice a year in Birmingham or Wembley. The British Vintage Wireless Society, (also c/o Sunrise Press) publishes bulletin newsletters and hold regular swapmeets and members' auctions.

Telephone Card Club of Great Britain, c/o Sandie Ford, PO Box 708, London SE25 4WE. Tel: 0181 654 5650.

The Vintage Wireless Museum, Dulwich, London. Tel: 0181 670 3667

SPECIALIST SHOPS AND SERVICES

VJ Bartlett and Sons, 14 Middle Street, Southampton SO14 6FX13. Kim-John Webb's clock and watch repairers and restorers.

Early Technology, 84 West Bow, Edinburgh, EH1 2HH. Tel: 0131 226 1132. Supplies parts for restoring anything that might come under the heading of early technology, from ways of making fire to computers.

Mike Smith Motoring Past, Chiltern House, Ashendon, Aylesbury, Buckinghamshire HP18 0HB. Tel: 01296 651 283. Mike runs four small autojumbles each year at Woburn Abbey, Abingdon, Luton and Aston Clinton. With his wife he also runs postcard fairs. With another partner he runs National Specialist Collectors' Fairs.

VW Collectibles, 15 St Cross Rd, Crondall, Farnham, Surrey GU10 5PQ. Tel: 01252 850761. Mobile 0411 936985. Fax: 01252 851542. Website: http;//www.ks.u-net.com/vwcollectibles
Sells inexpensive (£2–£40) new VW items by mail order. Send sae for list.

Worldwide Swatch Club. Tel: 01703 646834.

PUBLICATIONS
Go Great Western by R B Wilson (David and Charles). First published in the 1970s, re-issued in 1987. Might still be in print, or try secondhand bookshops and libraries.

Historic Televisions and Video Recorders by Michael Bennett Levy (available from Early Technology, 84 West Bow, Edinburgh, EH1 2HH, £14.95 inc. p&p).

International Telephone Cards (ITC) Magazine, 42 Phoenix Court, Hawkins Rd, Colchester, Essex CO2 8JY, UK. Tel: 01206 791734. Fax 01206 791736.

TV is King by Michael Bennett Levy (available from Early Technology, 84 West Bow, Edinburgh, EH1 2HH, £16 inc. p&p).

Volks World (UK) and *Hot VWs* (USA), are magazines available in newsagents which have regular coverage of collectable VW items.

Watch and Clock Making and Repairing by W J Gazeley (Robert Hale).

Chapter Seven ~ In Print

COLLECTORS' CLUBS, SOCIETIES AND MUSEUMS
The Enid Blyton Society, Ty Bryn Cragg Drive, Ben Rhydding, Ilkley, West Yorkshire. LS29 8BE.
Write for details of meetings and newsletter.

Cartophillic Society of Great Britain. Tel: 01225 704 839.

The Ephemera Society, 8 Galveston Road, Putney, London SW1. Tel: 0181 874 3363. Send sae for membership details.

Museum of Advertising & Packaging, The Albert Warehouse, Gloucester Docks, Gloucester GL1 2EH. Tel: 01452 302309. A history of the consumer society, much of Robert Opie's collection is housed here.

The Beatrix Potter Society, Secretary, Marian Werner, 32 Etchingham Park Road, Finchley, London N3 2DT. Tel: 0181 346 8031.

SPECIALIST SHOPS AND SERVICES
Book Conserver and Restorer, Cyril Formby 19–21 Market Place, Ramsbottom, Bury, Lancashire, BL0 9AJ. Tel: 01706 825771. Open Monday to Friday, 8am–noon, 1–4.30pm.

Bookmark, Fortnight, Wick Down, Broad Hinton, Swindon, Wiltshire, SN4 9NR. Tel: 01793 731693. Mail order service, for children's books and annuals. Send sae for free catalogue.

Institute of Paper Conservation (IPC), Leigh Lodge, Leigh, Worcester WR6 5LB. Tel: 01886 832323.
Can supply names of local conservers.

Out of print book service, Twiggers, 11 Fairmead Road, Shinfield, Reading RG2 9DL. Tel: 0118 988 2001. Fax: 0118 988 5416. Free preliminary search, £3 for extended search. No obligation, but can buy at cost of book plus p&p.

Society of Bookbinders, Chairman Tony Ward, 16 Latimer Drive, Calcot, Reading RG31 7AP. Send sae for membership details.

PUBLICATIONS
Book and Magazine Collector (The Publisher, Diamond Publishing Group Ltd, 43-5 St Mary's Rd, Ealing, London W5 5RQ). Published third Friday of the month.

Christmas Cards for the Collector by Arthur Blair (Batsford).

Collecting Books by Catherine Porter (Miller's, £19.99).

Collecting Children's Books compiled by *Book and Magazine Collector Magazine* (Priceguide, £19.95).

Discovering Christmas Customs and Folklore by Margaret Baker (Shire Publications, £3.95).

Mazawattee Tea by Diana James (The Pentland Press Limited, 1 Hutton Close, South Church, Bishop Auckland, Durham, £10).

The 1930s Scrapbook by Robert Opie (New Cavendish).

The 1950s Scrapbook by Robert Opie (New Cavendish).

Packaging Source Book by Robert Opie (McDonald Orbis, £20).

Picture Postcard Monthly, 15 Debdale Lane, Keyworth, Nottingham, NG12 5HT. Tel: 0115 937 4079 or 0115 937 6197. Stella Blazier's favourite magazine. Regular monthly publication for collectors of old and modern postcards, prices mentioned in articles throughout.

The Wartime Scrapbook by Robert Opie (New Cavendish).

Index

Acknowledgements

Special Thanks

To the collectors featured in this book who have been so generous with their time and knowledge. Though my name appears on the cover it has been a joint venture between us. Thanks also extend to the dealers and collectors I have learned from and shared good times with over the years, especially Annie Kay and Mary Mulroy of Salford and the staff at Christie's South Kensington who have been helpful and kind, above and beyond the call of duty.

To Two Four Productions for their help in the preparation of this book, in particular Jill Lourie, who trusted *ka communications* with this project, and Sadie Hennessey who nurtured the book during the early stages. Thanks also to Emma Tait at Boxtree for her forthright professionalism and sensitivity and to Slaney Begley for her positive, perceptive attitude, skill and hard work.

To the two people who worked with me on this book: my close colleague Gill Adams, whose professional and personal qualities I value more than words can say; and the resourceful Beth Hooper, who researched with intelligence while keeping track of the paperwork.

Last, but not least, to Mum, Dad, Auntie Joy, Lucy and Vic, for the love, understanding and unflinching support that makes everything possible.

Photographic Credits

The collector of each piece is given followed, in brackets, by the photographer.

t = top, b = bottom, l = left, r = right

contents: Veral Marshall (Ed Schneider), Juliette Edwards (Ed Schneider), Michelle Morgan (Ed Schneider), Major Donald Welsh (Ed Schneider), Christopher Butler (Ed Schneider), Kim-John Webb (Ed Schneider), David Cox (Ed Schneider); 7 Two Four Productions; 8 Isobel Whatrup (Ed Schneider); 10 Veral Marshall (Ed Schneider); 11 Simon Khachadourian (Ed Schneider); 12 Veral Marshall (Ed Schneider); 13 Richard Lowe; 14–15 Simon Khachadourian (Ed Schneider); 15 Simon Khachadourian (Ed Schneider); 16 Michelle Morgan (Ed Schneider); 17 Jenny Hunt (Ed Schneider); 18 Jenny Hunt (Ed Schneider); 20–1 Isobel Whatrup (Ed Schneider); 21t Isobel Whatrup (Ed Schneider), 21b Isobel Whatrup (Ed Schneider); 22 Anneka Reay; 23 Edward Bramah; 24 Chrissie Kravchenko (Ed Schneider); 26 Veral Marshall (Ed Schneider); 27 Veral Marshall (Ed Schneider); 28 Juliette Edwards (Ed Schneider); 29 Nick Tait and Ian Johnson (Ed Schneider); 30 Lucy Kravchenko (Ed Schneider); 31 The Antique Clothing Store (Ed Schneider); 33 Christine Hall; 34–5 Nicola Lynes (Ed Schneider); 35 Christine Hall (Ed Schneider); 36 Juliette Edwards (Ed Schneider); 37 Emma Tait (Ed Schneider); 38 Juliette Edwards (Ed Schneider); 39tl Juliette Edwards (Ed Schneider), 39tr Juliette Edwards (Ed Schneider), 39b Juliette Edwards (Ed Schneider); 40 Brenda Mathews (Ed Schneider); 41 Kim-John Webb (Ed Schneider); 42 Kim-John Webb; 43 Chris McGill (Ed Schneider); 44 Ann Louise Luthi (Ed Schneider); 45 Emma Tait (Ed Schneider); 46 Ann Louise Luthi (Ed Schneider); 47tl Ann Louise Luthi (Ed Schneider), 49tr Ann Louise Luthi (Ed Schneider), 49b Ann Louise Luthi (Ed Schneider); 48 Michelle Morgan (Ed Schneider); 49 Mike Wilson; 50 Chris McGill (Ed Schneider); 52–3 Nick Bennett (Ed Schneider); 53 Nick Bennett (Ed Schneider); 54 Nick Bennett (Ed Schneider); 55 Nick Bennett (Ed Schneider); 56 Michelle Morgan (Ed Schneider); 57t Michelle Morgan (Ed Schneider); 57b Michelle Morgan (Ed Schneider); 59t Malcolm Dickie (Ed Schneider); 59b Malcolm Dickie (Ed Schneider); 60 Helen Kelleher (Ed Schneider); 61 Shirley Abrey (Ed Schneider); 62 Shirley Abrey (Ed Schneider); 63t Shirley Abrey (Ed Schneider), 63b Shirley Abrey (Ed Schneider); 64 David Miles; 65 Christopher Butler (Ed Schneider); 66 Major Donald Welsh (Ed Schneider); 69 Angela Tait and Kate Briggs (Ed Schneider); 70–1 Michael Ellis (Ed Schneider); 72 Margaret Tyler (Ed Schneider); 74 Angela Tait and Kate Briggs (Ed Schneider); 76 Major Donald Welsh (Ed Schneider); 77 Major Donald Welsh (Ed Schneider); 78 Jonathon Cartwright (Ed Schneider); 80 Mary Price (Ed Schneider); 81 Mary Price (Ed Schneider); 82 Chrissie Kravchenko (Ed Schneider); 85 Ann Atkins; 86 Ann Atkins; 88 Christopher Butler (Ed Schneider); 89 Christopher Butler (Ed Schneider); 91 Christopher Butler (Ed Schneider); 92 Emma Tait (Ed Schneider); 93 Margaret Tyler (Ed Schneider); 94 Margaret Tyler (Ed Schneider); 94–5 Margaret Tyler (Ed Schneider); 95 Margaret Tyler (Ed Schneider); 96 Angela Tait (Ed Schneider); 98–9 Christopher Butler (Ed Schneider); 99 Christopher Butler (Ed Schneider); 100 Jonathon Cartwright (Ed Schneider); 102 Angela Tait and Kate Briggs (Ed Schneider); 105 Stella Mitchell; 106 Julian Litten (Ed Schneider); 107t Julian Litten (Ed Schneider), 107bl Julian Litten (Ed Schneider), 107br Julian Litten (Ed Schneider); 109 Kim-John Webb (Ed Schneider); 110 Colin Hill; 111t Colin Hill, 111b Colin Hill; 112 David Dunning (Ed Schneider); 113t David Dunning (Ed Schneider), 113b David Dunning (Ed Schneider); 114 Kenneth Tait (Ed Schneider); 116–17 David Coan (Ed Schneider); 117 David Coan (Ed Schneider); 118 Kim-John Webb (Ed Schneider); 120 Kim-John Webb (Ed Schneider); 121 Kim-John Webb (Ed Schneider); 122 Roman Piekarski; 125 Gerald Baker; 126 Mike Smith; 128 David Cox; 129 Chris McGill (Ed Schneider); 131 Stella Blazier (Ed Schneider); 132 Diana James (Ed Schneider); 133 Leapfrog Press Ltd (Ed Schneider); 134 David Coan (Ed Schneider); 136 Diana James (Ed Schneider); 137t Diana James (Ed Schneider), 137b Diana James (Ed Schneider); 139 Judith Howard (Ed Schneider); 140–1 David Cox (Ed Schneider); 141 David Cox (Ed Schneider); 142 Kris Kyriakou (Ed Schneider); 143 Emma Tait (Ed Schneider); 145 Kris Kyriakou (Ed Schneider); 147 Gillian Baverstock.